"Doing our Bit for the Country"
Walter Pounds M.M.

*Letters sent home while a soldier in W.W.1
Awards and Diary notes*

RENATE
Hope you enjoy the testimoneal
to my father   Derrick P.W. Pounds
OCT 17, 2014

Mr. Derrick P.W. Pounds Eng

Cover
Walter Pounds M.M. stalking grouse on the moors with a springer spaniel.

ISBN: 1490312196
ISBN-13: 9781490312194

© 2013 Mr. Derrick P.W. Pounds Eng
Contact email: *Derrick.Pounds@sympatico.ca*

Contents

Introduction...v

Letters Walter Pounds M.M. sent home during WWI.........1

Army Records for Walter Pounds M.M. 29

Awards received by Walter Pounds M.M. 31

The Ratcliff estate in Newton Solney 33

Training Dogs..37

Pheasant and Partridge shoots..........................39

Hunting Rabbits using Ferrets..........................43

Hunting more Vermin 45

Fishing on the River Dove 47

Ratcliffs' other hunting and fishing properties........51

Special Constable Walter Pounds 53

Growing Vegetables 57

Planting trees and evergreen shrubs 59

Father's other notes 61

Walter Pounds M.M. and his Pound_ ancestors 77

The passing of Walter Pounds M.M. at age Ninety-Six 81

INTRODUCTION

Walter Pounds M.M. was born January 11, 1895, in the Bee Hive, Church Lane, Newton Solney, Derbyshire, England, and attended the village primary school until age thirteen. On January 11, 1908, he started work first as a stable boy on the Ratcliff estate, becoming assistant gamekeeper before being sent to learn about pheasant rearing as a trainee gamekeeper on King George V's estate at Windsor Great Park, living in Englefield Green, Surrey. While tending pheasants in the Windsor woods just before the outbreak of WWI, he watched a nephew of Queen Victoria land a small German monoplane in Windsor Great Park and take off after a brief visit, returning to Germany. He enlisted in the army on December 2, 1914.

Walter Pounds M.M. served his country in both world wars, as a soldier for four and a quarter years in WWI (ID tag #56258) and as a special police sergeant in WWII. He fought with the British Army's Royal Garrison Artillery in France and Belgium from 1915 to 1918, was seriously wounded twice, shelled, gassed, bombed by aircraft, and subjected to liquid fire. He received campaign ribbons and four medals, including the Military Medal (M.M.), the British Army's second-highest commendation for valor. He convalesced at the Caird Rest Hospital in Dundee, Scotland, for four weeks after suffering head and shoulder shrapnel wounds at Ypres (Leper, Flanders) on June 3, 1916, while serving with the Seventy-First Heavy Artillery battery. Returning to the battlefields in France, his "285" siege battery gun was blown up on May 6, 1917, by a shell. Buried by debris and hit by shrapnel, Walter Pounds suffered an upper leg wound requiring weeks of convalescence at Cornelia Hospital, Poole, Dorset, before he again volunteered for service in France. Transcripts of thirty letters he wrote to his mother and father while he was serving in the British Army during the First World War, 1914–1918, follow.

LETTERS WALTER POUNDS M.M. SENT HOME DURING WWI

Several letters were written on the battlefields in Flanders and France, and others were written while in hospitals recovering from war wounds and during training in the cavalry, when teams of six horses were used to pull four-wheeled gun carriages. His war wounds in 1916 included a piece of a shell lodged in his skull behind his right ear, the folded skin covering the shrapnel being clearly visible throughout his life after a haircut. Doctors determined that it would have been too life-threatening to attempt removal of the shrapnel. In spite of this, my father never applied for an army pension based on his brother's experience. Walter Pounds's brother Bill lost a leg in WWI and received a small pension. However, after the war the equivalent of this pension amount was taken off Bill's wages every week. Walter Pounds believed that any pension money due for his war wounds would also have been deducted from his wages that in 1935 were two pounds, fifteen shillings per week.

LETTER FROM WALTER POUNDS 56258 HEAVY BATTERY RGA, 12 GRUNVILLE PARK, LEWISHAM, LONDON, WRITTEN IN 1915

Dear Mother & Father

Just a few lines to you to thank you for letter and also the PO. I will send you the money Wednesday or Thursday. We are having Gun

Drill now and learning the different parts about it including no firing as we practice with blank shells. It is just like real firing only there is no bang but we have a great deal to learn yet but they are teaching us into it now they are trying to make our company look the smartest. We get plenty of juice jelly peas first thing in the morning. We do not expect to stay at this house long as we hear we are going into huts in about 1 month time. I was sorry to hear Father has been ill but hoping he is feeling better. I must now close with more later. Love Walter

Letter from Walter Pounds 56258 circa March 1915 located at 131 Heavy Battery, Charlton Park, Woolwich, London

Dear Mother

Just a few lines received letter and cash quite safe. Sorry I cannot come this weekend as I am on Guard Saturday Evening so cannot get my Pass if on Duty. But may come the week after all-being well anyway you can expect me this next fortnight for if I do not come now I shall not get the chance. We are having a little rain today but nothing to speak about we can do with a little to tag the dust. We have had it so hot as just a few of us made our bed outside. It is A1 outdoor treatment only the worst of it you generally get someone kind enough to try and pull you out but we get used to all that.

The pay Master here heard from Dover yesterday and cannot get any allowance as you were not depending on me. I may write to Dover yet the pay Master wanted me to put. I do not think it hardly worthwhile. I told the pay Master you was not depending on me but I was only helping to keep you as Father's wages was not enough. That Devil what came and seen you was too nosy. I can keep on allowing you the 3s & 6p. If I care to put I do not know whether I shall anyway I will keep on allowing it till I come home then we can see. If I had known I would not have mentioned Windsor Park but then there is always some one kind enough to tell them <u>Different</u> I hardly think conscription will come but they may pick anyone they think fit for the Army. I expect West will have to go. I shall have to come and give Bill a lesson or two he should have joined when I did he would be an old soldier like me with six months service. It seems like I had got six years in the RGA I have got out about lately. We had a draft go from Woolwich last week to the base. We do a little rough riding now. It's great to get astride.

Must close with best of love.
Walter

Hoping you are all well. Will write to Bill later, rather busy.

LETTER FROM WALTER POUNDS 56258 MONDAY CIRCA MARCH 1915.....FROM FORT ELSON

Dear Mother and Dad

Just a few lines to you in Hast hoping this finds you all well at Home. This leaves me fine in Health but rather downhearted at not getting leave before leaving for France. We have tried our hardest to get leave but it was no use so you can bet the Troops are dissatisfied they would not even allow us twenty four hours off and we have only been allowed out four hours a day. We are giving them all a good booing tomorrow as we leave here for they have treated us like dogs and most of the Boys have been out to France once and volunteered for the draft. I have myself to blame but must put up with it now. We leave here early tomorrow morning for Southampton and across tomorrow night so by the time you get this I shall be well on my way. I will soon forget peace when I get out of England but it is rotten Hard Luck. I expect the Girl will be over Home sometime at Easter so just give Her a good time. I will drop you a line from Southampton and when I land. I have not had a letter here and I expect we shall be away before the Post comes tomorrow but I hope you got my Parcels safe and I hope you get the allotment of nine pence a day I am making to you it starts from the second of April. If you have any trouble with it drop me a line and I will see the Officer the other side but I think it will be alright. I will write to Bill when I get settled down and I hope I have the luck to drop across his Battalion. I will keep my eyes open for Him. I hope the weather improves before long we have had snow here today Monday. I must now be ringing off as I have to rise early tomorrow. I hope you all keep well while I am in France and hope for the War to Finish so I can finish with this lot and get Back Home.

Love to all
Walter XXX

PS I have been sharpening my teeth ready for the luscious biscuits. We will be all dressed up and nowhere to go tomorrow. I'll have to get a donkey in this rig out. Bats weighing half a ton

LETTER CARD FROM WALTER POUNDS WRITTEN AT SOUTHAMPTON DOCKS

Dear Mother

Just a few lines hoping this finds you well as it leaves me A1. You will be surprised I have not gone yet but owing to some of the boys over staying their leave we were delayed a day or so but we go tonight from Southampton. We arrived here at 12 o'clock noon & are having to wait till night rather a bad job for we cannot get off the docks. There are several Regiments going in the same troop ship. Hope it is calm as we shall all be seasick. We see a lot of German prisoners today in Southampton; we did not half give them a hooting. I must now close hoping this finds you all well.

Love to all
Walter

Letter from Walter Pounds 56258 Thursday April 1915 at #12 Camp, Le Havre, B.E.F., France

Dear Mother & Father

Just a few lines letting you know we arrived safe in France, we arrived Le Havre first thing this morning after being on the boat all night. We had exciting times on board but not much sleep. When we landed we had a 6 mile walk to where we are camped. We are under canvas now. I shall be as long as we are here we do not expect to stay here long but are going further up the line so you may write by return of post. We are roughing it on Bully beef and biscuits which is rather bracing to the teeth. I must now close hoping this finds you all well as it leaves me in the best.

Much love Walter

Letter from Walter Pounds dated Friday 30th December 1915 71st Heavy Battalion, RGA 9th Brigade, B.E.F. France

Dear Mother & Dad

Just a few lines hoping this finds you all well at home. I am pleased to hear your hand is getting better & hope you will soon be better again.
Thanks so much for the writing paper & also for the letter which I received safe it landed here on the 29th December. I shall be set up for a short time. You still keep having these noted weddings at Newton Solney they seem as if they are all getting married is it to escape Lord Derby's scheme. I think something must be upsetting them every body has took a fancy to having a war wedding. I think I shall have to get leave and get married (What Hopes).
I am pleased to see Bill has joined for he would be the talk of the place if he had not done though I hope he will not come here for I want the War to finish before he has completed his training. I expect he will find just a little change to being at home but he will soon get used to

that for it is not bad soldering in England for you have somewhere dry to sleep. He told me he was going to try and join the same lot as me. I don't think he can beat it but he has his own fancies. I hear from F.Dickes he told me he had been and passed & also drawn the soldier pay there is no doubt Lord Derby's scheme has roused a few of them. We have been having very hot times out here but thank God no one has got killed in our Battery though we have had some near squeaks. We had two hot days the Saturday & Sunday before Xmas we were at it day & night & early on the Sunday morning they tried to break through our lines but failed though the Dirty Devils used gas we all had a little of it for the gases was upon us before we had time to get our helmets but no one had it very bad. It made our eyes sour but if it had not been for gas helmets we should have all been killed. I expect you see the account in the papers.

I expect you had a decent Xmas at home. We did not have ours until the 27th December for we were on Duty. We did not have a bad day on the 27th we had plenty of puddings but I hope I spend the next one in England. We had a good diner Xmas day bully beef & biscuits but I am feeling in the best on it & getting quite fat (I don't think). I have got quite a decent job when we are not firing observing for German Aeroplanes which we get plenty of round this quarter. They are very fond of dropping bombs on Batteries if they can get a chance though they get it pretty hot from our anti aircraft guns when they come our way. Love Walter

LETTER FROM WALTER POUNDS 56258 WITH THE RGA FIGHTING 1916 NEAR YPRES

Dear Mother

Just a line in hast to you letting you know I am quite safe after the Battle we have had here this last week.
I think I told you we were on a short rest but it only lasted a few day as we had quick orders to come back to the firing line & I can tell you we have had a hot time of it and lost 600 yards of trenches but I think we have got most of them back again for the Artillery shelled them out

of it. We had the order to get back one afternoon and the whole of the 17 miles we had to walk at a fast rate and the whole of the way it poured with rain. When we got to our position we were like drowned rats we did not land until 1:30 in the morning & all that night we had to be firing & all the next night. We have only had one night in bed this week & then we had had to sleep fully dressed they did not use gas this time but liquid fire. It has been a hot time. We are expecting another clash any day now but I think we shall hold them.

We have had several air raids this last day we only had 10 German planes over this morning & all today we have had plenty of fighting in the Air as well as down below. It is a devil out here for mud lately but today sunny. I only wish it would keep like it for a week or so.

This letter will be posted in England as one of my Pals is on leave in England I wish I was coming with him as I am fed up with the life out here. It is a regular tramps life & we have no fires to have a warm by but we keep on smiling as long as we are doing our bit for the country.

It makes you feel rather sorry for this country to see the wreck of the place, the fields around our guns are just like a quarry for it is full of shell holes & they smashed some of dugouts in the other night. We have had a few of our lads killed & others died of wounds but I think it lucky for any of us to be alive.

Our position is just outside the town of Ypres. I expect you often see the name in the papers we are about 50 yards from the main Calais road of which the Germans have so many times to get for. If we let them through here they would have a straight run to Calais but they have something to do to get through though we had a job hold them the other week.

So just look out for an attack around Ypres and hill 60 because I will be in them.

Must now close.
Hoping this finds you all well as it leaves me in the best.
Love Walter

Mr. Derrick P.W. Pounds Eng

Letter from Walter Pounds written in June 1916 at Caird Rest Hospital, Dundee, Scotland.

Dear Mother & Dad

Just a few lines letting you know I am in Scotland rather a quick shift. I left hospital Coumuroi in France on the 20th at two in the morning and landed at this hospital on the 21st. I am feeling much better but still in bed my head is doing fine & I have had the stitches taken out but my head feels more like a Jam cover for I had the nerves cut on the right side during the operation. A piece of the shell from my head went down the side of my neck and slid further fracturing my shoulder but the stiffness has almost left the shoulder now. I expect it has found a quiet spot they are leaving it in. It has been X-rayed at the line of my head but it is not dangerous. We had quite a decent journey coming across the channel. We landed at Dover and it was a treat to see old England again. It is great comfort in the hospital train they do not shake a bit. We came by the NWR so did not come through the Midlands. I am quite a decent way from Burton-on-Trent again but I do not mind anywhere bar Belgium. I see the Battle of Ypres is still going on. We had it hellish for two days and a night we had not left our Guns up to when I got wounded we had 15 gunners wounded when I got wounded so I don't know how the boys got on that were left. It was pretty hard work on our Gun which I left and shells were flying round in all directions. I must now close will write a longer letter later do not worry for I am A1 here and having the best. I hope to get up in a day or so. It is rather boring in bed especially when you have not been used to it. I shall get 10 days leave when I do leave here so that will not be too bad. Hoping you are all well at home, write soon and please send any letters on to me.

Much love Walter 56258 Gunner Pounds, Royal Garrison Artillery

Letters Walter Pounds M.M. Sent Home During WWI

LETTER 26/6/16 FROM CAIRD REST HOSPITAL, DUNDEE, SCOTLAND

Dear Mother & Dad

Just a few lines letting you know I am getting on A1 but still in bed and time goes rather slow. I am glad to hear you are all feeling well at home and sorry to hear of your letter being lost for I have not received them. I heard from my pal in France and they have found my small book and pay book and are forwarding on to my home address so you might send them on when they arrive. I heard from them they are still having a savage time and had five more wounded after I got wounded. I did not see any of them after I left the dressing station but I down to France in the hospital train there was wounded all over the place that day. You could not walk down the communication trenches for dead men blown to pieces. Most of the men I was with were Canadians. We are having a decent time here we had some Scots lasses to sing to us the other afternoon we quite enjoyed ourselves. We are expecting another one tomorrow. We could not get any better attention in any other hospital as we get here. It is just a matter of luck where you land up so we have some Scotsmen in this hospital but I don't mind where I am so long as it is away from Ypres. I have not heard from (brother) Bill only twice since I have been out there you had better send his address on and I will write to him. I am glad to hear he is still in Ireland otherwise I expect he would be going out to France very soon. We hear they have made an advance along the whole British Front. I hope it is true as it may shorten the war there is plenty of rumours of the war finishing soon but I think it will go on another winter as the Huns are very strong on the Western front. As regards aeroplanes they are better than us we used to have a German plane come and fire on us with his machine gun and several times they dropped bombs on us. We used to see plenty of fighting in the air when the weather was good sometimes we would get there (their) planes and sometimes the reverse sound. Where we were was a terrible place for much in the winter we could not get our Ammunition wagons within 400 yards of the Guns so we had to carry it in. It was a good job I can tell you and rather hard work through mud and shell holes. We dare not have lights and you had to feel your way about and if you happen to fall across a shell hole you can bet you had a good bath but it came in rather useful at times for lice. I never see anything like it everyone was walking and we could not get a change of washing so we used to take our clothes off and give them a straffing and then dry brush them. You can tell we used to see life a little but for all the hardships we had very little sickness. I don't think I had a cold to speak of all winter and it was impossible to keep dry. Next time you write you might send me 10 shillings for when I get out for I have had no pay since the middle of May. When we get fit to go out we are allowed out so many hours a day and we can go to the theatre when we like so I am longing to get up. I heard from W. Taylor the other day the first letter I have since I see him in France he lost my address so sent it to you first . He is quite well but I don't think he cares for the spot much and the weather there has been very hot. I must close now hoping this finds you all well as it leaves me feeling much better. Has West been called up yet I think it is about time some of them are trying to shirk it. They should hear what the boys think of them in France.

Much love to all, Walter (Pounds) 26/6/16

Letter written 8th August 1916 by Walter Pounds at Fort Brookhurst, No. 2 Depot, Gosport, Portsmouth.

Dear Mother & Dad

Just a few lines I arrived safe at Gosport. I am feeling rather home sick and also tired for I did not land in till 3:30 this morning. I think I stand a good chance of being in England for a few months. I was in front of the doctor this morning and he marked me a D care which means home service for six months but he may alter it next time I go. Hope not there are plenty of troops here I never see so many and plenty of conscripts. I must now close hoping you are all well as it leaves me not too bad. You might forward any letters on to me.

Love Walter

Letters Walter Pounds M.M. Sent Home During WWI

Letter written by Walter Pounds 56258 on 20th August 1916 at Fort Brockhurst, No. 2 Depot RGA, Gosport, Portsmouth

Dear Mother & Dad

Just a few lines thanking you for your letter received 20th August 1916 and also the two letters they are not the answered letters I expected as one of them was from W. Taylor from Solinskey and the other from France. I am pleased to hear that Bill has arrived I wish I had known he was coming I would have seen one of the Officers for leave but it is too late now. I expect he is having a good time at home I wish I was there but I may see him before I go to France again. I hope you are having good weather as it is A1 here. I expect Bill is just giving you his Army life. I can just fancy him telling the tale it wanted me there to tell him the tale. I could just give him a few tips as regards Army life I expect Dick is looking after him. I have had a rotten week this week had to stay in Barracks all week as I have been on Fire Picket quite an easy job to do but it is hard life for me to be penned in. I am still D3 but feeling not too bad. I was surprised to hear West had (Next page missing) .... so must not complain. I see you had that grand wedding. I expect it was a swanky affair for they are rather swanky people. I don't think Bill gets on all that well with F. at Bladon he's a silly kid for letting him boss him about. I know I would not. Bill tells me Duke Woollen was over he has not joined the army yet. I heard from Arthur Hall the other week, he is getting on well. I am writing him back today they are having a decent time from what he says he is trying to get on as shoeing Smith with his buddy. I t is not a bad job if he passes we have some in our Battery learning. I know they get pay for it.

Bill tells me Dad is trying to get Bedford's job I hope he gets it as it would be much better for you. I must now close hoping this finds you all well as this leaves me in the best of health. I hope the mislaid parcel arrives safe.

Much love Walter

PS we had a grand march past this morning after Church parade about 12 hundred of us, some think like a little service.

Two Post Cards written by Walter Pounds 56258 Monday October 1916 while at the Bostall Heath Camp, RGA, Abby Wood, Kent

Dear Mother

Just a few lines hoping you are all well at home as this leaves me A1. We have landed at our destination and it is not too bad. I may be home on leave in a week or so if I have any luck. You might write back by return of Post and also send me 5 shillings as funds are low. Hoping this finds you in the best.

Walter

PS I heard from Bill he is a little nearer the firing line

Second Postcard both time/date stamped 9:30pm Woolwich SE 12th October 1916

Dear Mother

I shall be home Friday 13th for a few days leave. I don't suppose I shall get in very early as I shall be able to get away from here till six o'clock but I shall lose no time once I start so hoping you are all well as this leaves me fine. Love to all Walter

The last two pages of letter by Walter Pounds from Bostall Heath Camp

…I may be one of the lucky ones but I do not bother where they send me now as I don't expect any more leave just yet. I am glad the bait I set for Mr. Fox caught him napping. I expect Dad has set them again but tell him he wants to move them a few yards away from where I put them then he may pick up another one if there are any more. I was sorry to hear of Mrs Wooley and being so young. I expect they are fine and upset

about it at Newton. I must now ring off as news are rather scarce ... here so hoping this finds you all well at home as this leaves me fine. Just ask FD to write he is rather long winded.

Love to all, Walter, Bostall Heath Camp

LETTER WRITTEN BY WALTER POUNDS TUESDAY DECEMBER...1916...BOSTALL CAMP, HUT NO. 4

Dear Mother & Dad

Just a few lines hoping this finds you all well at home as this leaves me feeling much better. I have almost got rid of the cold but it wants a lot of shifting. I heard from Bill he asked me to ask you to write as he not heard from you for a long time they are back now for six weeks rest but they have had a hot time of it. He was in the charge that was made on that foggy morning. They caught the Huns all asleep in their dugouts and took 1,000 prisoners which was good work but the worst of it they had to hold the German front line of trenches which they had captured for five days before they were relieved so they could do with a little rest but they will be lucky if they stay back for six weeks. He is keeping well but the weather is rotten for them. We are not getting Xmas leave from what we have heard today no leave to be granted to any troops but we cannot help it. I had a fine weekend a Pal of mine from France was home in London for 8 days so I had the weekend with him. I expect you know the one I often used to spend the weekends with him before he went to France. Poor kid he had to go back last night. Jolly rough to have to go back again after once coming home he says the mud out there is terrible he was just about covered in it but was looking well. I heard from FD he told me Lacey was ill. I am very sorry to hear it but I hope by now she is feeling better. I must now close hoping these few lines find you all well.

Love to all Walter

PS if you haven't written to Bill please Do so

Mr. Derrick P.W. Pounds Eng

Letter from Walter Pounds 56258 RGA Saturday January 14 1917 Bostall Heath Camp, Hut E II, Abbey Woods, Kent

Dear Mother & Dad

Many thanks for letter I received safe I was sorry to hear you had been ill in bed but I hope by now you are feeling much better and all at home. I have been rotten bad myself for four days. I got poisoned through eating tinned Fish but am feeling a lot better today Saturday but my skin is in a fine mess. I could hardly see for two days my face was so swollen now it is blistered and I have spots all over me but they are going away. No more tinned fish for me I thought I was going to snuff it on Thursday for my temperature was very high for I burned like a fire. I feel as if I had lice now from the itching. I have not heard from Bill since I returned but I am pleased you heard. I have written twice to him. I am glad he had a good time at Xmas and had plenty to eat for it is the main thing out there it will be a good job when it is finished so as all the boys can come home but I think the end is coming very soon I think this war loan will frill… Germany from all accounts it is going to be a great hassle and they have made a grand start it seems as if we are not short of cash.

They have sent several drafts to France from here lately but they have refused my name from all accounts they are sending all the fellows who have not been out and giving us a rest so I shall not worry the good weather comes being up here though it is not very exciting we have to drill Saturday afternoon now for we have to put all our time on training. I must now close hoping this finds you all well as this leaves me fair. I shall always remember my twenty second birthday.

Love to all Walter

Letters Walter Pounds M.M. Sent Home During WWI

Letter written by Walter Pounds 56258 Wednesday, March 7 1917 at the Hayeley Down Camp, 4th Reserve Battery RGA, Hut E 13, D Sub, Winchester

Dear Mother & Dad

Many thanks for letter received safe and hear you are all keeping well at Home. I hear from Bill today posted in France on the 3rd so rather quick in coming he is keeping A1 and is now going on a course of cooking for a few weeks which is much better than being in the ranks and should suite him. I heard from him two or three days ago but the letter had been delayed at Bostall he also sent me a photo of Albert Church which is pretty good that is where the advance started from last summer and there is heavy fighting in front of there now but we are making fine progress if we can hold them.

We are about the same old stuff here plenty of work and little food but keep smiling. I have not been out but one night since I came here so if I keep this up I shall have it pretty good but it is rather rotten staying in camp every night and getting no excitement in camp but I may get out a little when the light nights come along if I am here then when we have finished work and had tea it is dark so we get very little time for going out and we have to be in camp by ten. I am generally in bed by nine as it the best place for these huts are very cold and the weather had been cold and wet lately. We are on the top of a hill so get a good sea breeze and it is doing me fine as I feel A1 and getting fat on fresh air. I don't know how you get on for living but I know it must be hard for you. They have stopped the I.... from selling cake during the day so we cannot get a feed of cake until after five o'clock. I think if the war lasts much longer we shall all be starving.

We are getting the war bread and very coarse but I like it better than the other though it looks black it goes down A1. We have not had potatoes for weeks now we are having sweads, turnips instead anything to fill we have had what we call rabbit food that is watercress(oh we do like) but we shall have a few more losses in a day or so , so we shall be on bran mashes so the Boys say.

I expect Flo (Florence Hammond, whom he married 10th *May, 1919) has told you her brother is getting married at Easter they gave me an invitation but I shall not be able to get off so I could not promise as leave is hard to get but I think I will have to give him a present but I hardly know what to get what do you think would suit just give me advice for I have not had much to do with marriages I expect when they know I cannot get off (they will be offended) for they were looking forward to seeing me there. I know Flo was.*

I will have to …… I was surprised that Peter was over I expect Peter would like another go at the bottle but he will have to wait till next Xmas. F. Dickes is talking of joining again he will have to make hast or he will be too late some of them like talking about it but that is as far as they get they can do with them on the Western front. These men who have come up are afraid to death of facing the fighting they would pay £'s to get off drafts but they do not seem to wanted us to go out while they are holding back but I know if they asked for volunteers they would get plenty for we are fed up here. Hoping this finds you in the best and all at home.

Love to all, Walter

PS I have written back to Bill

LETTER WRITTEN BY WALTER POUNDS 56258 TUESDAY 12ᵀᴴ MARCH 1917 AT THE HAYELEY DOWN CAMP, 4ᵀᴴ RESERVE BATTERY RGA, HUT E 13,D SUB, WINCHESTER

Dear Mother & Dad

Many thanks for letter which I received safe. Sorry to hear Dad has been home on the sick list but I hope he is feeling better and able to turn out. I expect you have had the same weather as us down here for it has been for a week or more now "miserable" first snow, then rain, we have been just about washed away here and the ground being chalky makes it rotten getting about but after we have done work I do not bother going out so it bothers me very little. We have had good news here this week for

Letters Walter Pounds M.M. Sent Home During WWI

we hear we are shifting away from this camp but I do not know where we are bound for. I hope to goodness we move from this place for I am fed up with the district. It may only be a rumour but I hope it comes off. I am off drill for a week and helping with the cooking and getting the meals ready for the troops. It is hard work but I enjoy it better than being with horses. We have plenty of washing up to do for we have 750 troops each meal and they each have a plate and basin pie man and we have to wash them after them and scrub 36 tables besides cooking and getting different things ready but you can bet I look after no one trust me. We are living a lot cleaner than we have been doing for a Captain is in charge of the messing before they were having it any way no system and a lot of the food was getting sold outside the camp but they have kept a sharp eye on the Rations lately. We get tea and three luck biscuits at six o'clock in the morning and soup at half past seven at night so the troops are not complaining quite so much. We have to cut all bread up and butter it for them so you can guess we have some work to do in the course of the day but it passes the time away and you cannot go out at nights so it keeps the mind active. We had some photos taken today in the mess hut. If they come out any good I will get you one of them. Some of our Boys have gone on farm work today any ones who could plough had to hand their names in but I did not hand mine in though I think do little farm work but they are only going for a month and none of my Pals were going so I did not bother and they were not sending anyone around your way so I would be just as bad off as regards getting home and I do not think it is much of a go for you are attached to some company so it is like being under Army discipline and that's what I would like to get out of .Too many bosses don't suit me as I am apt to tell some of them my mind.

 I was very much surprised to hear of F. Dickes being married and I could hardly believe it when I read your letter and his reached me the same day. He does not say but very little in his letter only that he is married and living at home till he gets a house and that he will tell me all when he sees me. He does not even say he has had to get married but I think by his letter he seems very downhearted and I am very sorry for Frank and for his parents - but he seemed all right at Xmas don't you think. I wonder he has not got married sooner than this but they have kept it very dark but I hope they settle down together though I expect his Father feels it. I feel rather sorry for Mr. Dickes for he has had a deal of trouble lately and no doubt he will miss Frank at home for I know he was the upkeep of the home but I think Frank should have a little more sense than to go mad for a Girl like he has done. I think it was why he never Enlisted being too busy courting. It would have been better if he had enlisted for no doubt every one will look down on him a little. I am writing a letter back tonight to cheer him up a little so I will have to close hoping this finds you all well at home as this leaves me in the Best of health but the weather rotten.

Love to all Walter

PS Who was best Man at Frank's wedding? I may write again if I get the Photo this week for I will know this week if we are moving.

LETTER WRITTEN BY WALTER POUNDS 56258 SATURDAY MARCH 20, 1917 FROM 4TH RESERVE BATTERY RGA, HUT E 13 D SUB, HAYELEY DOWN CAMP, WINCHESTER

Dear Mother & Dad

Many thanks for letter received safe hoping these few lines find you all well at home as this leaves me A1 but for a cold the weather here has been terrible this last few days and we have had a deal of snow here and snow too the snow has not laid for a good job but when it did snow we knew all about it for the daylight was turned to darkness but after the snow had fallen the sun started to shine so you can tell it has been some funny weather. From the papers it has been a general thing and I expect it has hampered the troops out in France. They have been doing well lately but I think the worst has to come for the Germans are making a good retreat and no doubt they have strong positions to fall back on. Some people think the war will be over soon I sometimes think the same but the fighting still goes on and I expect will do so long as there is fighting in Germany. Once our troops reach Germany the fighting may slacken off but not while they hold Belgium and half of France and a good portion of Russia. I am out of the Cook House now when they found I was a trained Gun layer they soon fetched me out of it *and I am on the guns once again. I had a photo taken while I was in there but it has come out rather bad on account of the light but I will send one in this letter as they will do to look back <u>when</u> I am out of the Army. I was expecting leave when I wrote last but never came off as I expected it to do but I may get anytime. I have been trying hard to get home at Easter but things seem against me. I would have liked to have got to the Wedding of Florrie's Brother but owing to spotted fever breaking out at the Infantry Camp next to ours most of the leave is cancelled else by now I might have been on my way for France. None of our Boys have caught the disease yet but the fellows in the next camp have had some bad cases. We are all attending hospital here twice a day and gargling the throat and nose to keep the germs from spreading as it is very catching and if we miss going to the hospital we are for the O.C. or the Light Jump. I have not heard from Bill yet but he has hardly had time to answer my last letter but I hope he is keeping well this cold weather. I should think he will soon be having a leave. I hope FD is getting settled by now. I wrote and told him I was expecting leave I expect that is why he called I was surprised to hear of C. Brown joining up I expect he volunteered some hopes they are making these last joined troops go to France before us fellows although we are longing for a shift from here as it is terrible. I must now ring off. I am sending 16/ by this letter so I will have a little when I come on leave. Love to all at Home,*

Walter

P.S (when I get leave I will drop you a wire) Just look for Jack the Giant Killer on the back- we stood him on a box

Letter written by Walter Pounds Monday March 22nd, 1917, RGA, Hut B 13, D sub, Hayeley Down Camp

Dear Mother

Just a few lines in hast to you I am sending my riding trousers and spurs home for I am expecting to go to France any day. I volunteered for a draft being as the Boys I know did and I was to have come home Sunday till Wednesday. I passed the Doctor Saturday and packed my kit but Sunday morning the leave and the draft was cancelled for the time being some of the Boys who had long distance went Saturday night but were recalled Sunday morning. We think there is trouble in England somewhere for we are standing by waiting orders early Sunday morning and we had two Guns left here but where they went we do not know. A lot of the Infantry also left here early Sunday morning in a hurry too but we have not heard yet where the trouble is. We have had a lot of rumours but cannot believe them. Of course I may get leave yet but I am being on the safe side and sending some of my belongings home. If we hear any more I will send you a wire.

Much love to all. Walter

Wednesday March 24 1917 4 Reserve Battalion, Hayeley Down

We are leaving here tomorrow Thursday for Fort Brockhurst, Portsmouth. I may get leave from there but at present it is doubtful.

Love to all Walter

Letter written 26/4/17 by Gunner Walter Pounds, 56258, "285" Seige Battery, RGA, British Expeditionary Force, France

Dear Mother & Dad

Just a line thanking you for letter received 25th the address found me alright and glad to hear you are all keeping well at home. I hope by now you have heard from Bill I have wrote three letters since I landed here and have had no reply but I am hoping to get one and I hope he is alright and keeping well. I am trying my best to try and find out where he is I heard they were out of the trenches but I cannot get any time off to get a look around they have been around this part but I don't know if they are still here. I hope they are I may get a chance of seeing him but it is a hard job among so many troops if he has had my letter I should hear any day now. I have not heard from the Girl yet since leaving the base but letters often get delayed out here. I have not received the parcel yet but it should follow me on.

It has been fairly lively around here lately and we have had plenty of work in fact a little too much to please me. I have been rather unlucky and had two nights on working parties so sleep has been a thing of the past but we have to keep smiling and make the best of it. I may get back to my old Battery yet I hope so. I see by the letter you have heard from Dover you might let me know what the credit due was. You will get the 5 shillings and three pence every week now I see you put four and three pence in your letter but nine pence a day comes to five and three pence so that is what you should get. I would not bother to put any in the war loan and I think it is closed but you can transfer out of the bank into the loan at present but it is the bank with out you think better. The photos were taken on the night before leaving France and were sent on to my chums' home and from there to Bolton at present. I have not seen them so if they have come out alright. I shall have to have one of them sent down to you when I hear from Florry. I must now be closing as I do not get a deal of time off here; we are working from six till six without night work. Hoping this finds you all in the best at Home as this leaves me.

Love to all
XX Walter XX 285 Seige Battery, RGA,

CARD WRITTEN BY WALTER POUNDS 2ND MAY & CLEARED BY THE FIELD CENSOR ON 4TH MAY 1917

Dear Mother

Hoping this finds you all well at home as this leaves me fine. I heard from Bill today and he is keeping well. The weather is great out here lately.

Love to all
Walter

Mr. Derrick P.W. Pounds Eng

LETTER WRITTEN SUNDAY MAY 6ᵀᴴ 1917 WHILE SERVING IN FRANCE 286 SURGE BATTERY

Dear Mother & Dad

Many thanks letter received yesterday and glad to hear you have heard from Bill. I sent a card letting you know I had heard from him they are in the trenches now but I expect they will be out any time now. I am waiting to hear when they are out for I feel sure of seeing him when he comes out. The weather has been a treat here lately which makes it much better. I am glad you received the Back Pay I wrote for to Dover on landing here. I should have had it before leaving but came off in rather a hurry. I cannot get a line from Fred but he is still keeping well from your letter. He must be expecting to be called up from the papers they mean to have them all this summer. I expect Frank is still at home with his wife and if he has to go they will feel it at his home. I expect things must be hard living in England now things must be getting serious as they talk of having tickets but I hope this lot finishes before long at present it is fairly lively out here but the British and French are doing well but Fritze is fairly strong yet and seems to have plenty of shells to throw about but not quite as many as us for lately we have been giving him Hell. I must not stay any longer as I might be late and two days ago I received a punishment of two days pay stopped and two days field punishment for being ten minutes late on parade but I keep smiling it is my first crime since being in the Army and it was a simple offence six of us got the same punishment so we kept each other happy. I must now close hoping this finds you in the best of health as this leaves me in the best of health.

Love to all at Home
Walter

LETTER FROM WALTER POUNDS DATED MAY 10TH 1917 IN THE ST DENNIS TENT, CORNELIA HOSPITAL, POOLE, DORSET

Dear Mother & Dad

Just a few lines letting you know I am in Blighty once again. I was wounded on the 6th night 12:30am in the leg but making fine progress. I landed here this morning after being at Bourlogne Hospital from the 6th and from the look of things we are in for a good time and the Best of attention so you can bet I will be quite Happy here so do not worry about me. I must say I am very lucky to be here and all after what we went through on the sixth for Fritz gave our Battery a Hellish shelling and I thought we stood better chance of getting out of it for the Major of our Battery made us man the Guns throughout the whole of it and was not until our Gun got blown up that I was wounded. I got buried at the beginning of the strafe but only had a good shaking. I expect Bill will be surprised to hear I am in England for I expected to see him when he came out of the trenches for I was just behind him in the trenches they were in the support trenches in a wood in front of Hickebast near Ypres. I see one of Bills pals in Hospital and he knew Bill quite well and went over the top in the Somme offensive with Bill. I heard all about him from this chum of his he said Bill had got a fine job now and had finished going into the front line trenches. I must now close as I am feeling rather tired after the journey.

So with the best of love to all
From Walter.

LETTER FROM WALTER POUNDS M.M. WRITTEN MAY 14TH 1917 IN THE ST DENNIS MARQUE, CORNELIA HOSPITAL POOLE, DORSET

Dear Mother & Dad

Many thanks for letter I received this morning pleased to hear you are all keeping well at Home. This leaves me feeling a lot better but still in bed but the pain of my leg is getting A1 and the piece of shell was taken out in France. I did not have a lot of trouble for the shell has not fractured any bones, it seems quite a treat here and the weather is lovely. We are in large tents and it is very cool in bed here far better than being in a building and the beneing is AI. A few of the boys were torpedoed in coming across so they have rather a hard fight to get to England but only a few of them were drowned they always bring German prisoners across in the hospital ships now and put them in the bottom of the boat so they stand very little chance of escaping and the devils deserve it. The struggle out in France gets a deal fiercer and it a wonder that human nature stands what goes on out there right now and the end seems a long way off the British & French are doing fine but the Russians are at a stand still and by the looks of things they will have to lose or make peace with Germany but we must keep smiling. I have written to Bill from here he will be surprised to hear I am at Home. I wish he was here too. I must now be closing you might send me 5shillings by return as cigs are rather scarce and I have had no pay for a month so don't forget. Hoping this finds you all well as this leaves me getting on fine. I am looking forward to the 10 days leave.

Love to all xx Walter xx

LETTER WRITTEN BY WALTER POUNDS CIRCA MAY 1917 AT THE CLUNY RED CROSS HOSPITAL, SWANAGE, DORSET

Dear Mother & Dad

Just a few lines betting you know I am keeping well and still having a good time. I have been shifted to Cluny Red Cross Hospital now we landed here last night at eleven thirty owing to another batch of wounded coming into Poole we were transferred but I am smiling we have been having plenty of excitement at Poole. Yesterday we went to the Bournemouth Theatre and had a good time. I was at a whist drive in the week and won the first prize in the Ladies we had no lady partners so we had to wear roses. I score 118 tricks in 15 games so was not a bad score the next to me was 105. I had a box of 100 cigarettes and a tin of tobacco so was a good prize. I heard from Bill two days ago I don't think his punishment is at all bad and he does not seem to mind but he has lost his staff job. I must now close hoping to hear from you.

Love Walter

P.S. Please send me 5 shillings

LETTER FROM WALTER POUNDS 3 COMPANY, HUT 21, 39 SOUTH CAMP, RA COMMAND DEPOT

Dear Mother & Dad

Just a few lines hoping this finds you all well at Home as this leaves me A1. I have been expecting a line from you. I hope you received my letter safe. I heard from Bill today and he is doing A1 and gets up of a afternoon which is a good job but I expect he is pretty weak yet but he will soon get strong again once he gets about a little. Camp life is about the same and we get plenty of mucking about which I do not like for this is supposed to be a convalescence Camp but it gets more like a training depot. We get it much harder now I am in Division 11 A. I may be here only three more weeks but I do not mind what they do with me. I spent the worst Bank Holiday I ever spent as I never had a cent after Sunday night. I only received four shillings last week and out of that by the time I had a good feed it took very little.

Will you please send me 5 shillings when you write again?
Hoping to hear from you soon

Love to all.
Walter

Mr. Derrick P.W. Pounds Eng

Letter written by Walter Pounds 56258 Tuesday......3 Company, stationed at 39 Camp Hut 17, RA Command Depot

Dear Mother & Father

Many thanks for your letter of Saturday last and also P.O. which I was pleased to receive. I was never so short of money since being in the Army this last three weeks. I have only been drawing four shillings a week and by the time pay day has come I have been in debt. I cannot get my right pay here and up to now I have not drawn my back pay. I have not much to draw but they do not seem in any hurry to pay back money here. I expect they are keeping it till the war is over. I see they still keep talking of paying us the extra money. I hope it comes off quick for I can do with a raise. I am paying the Doctor a visit tomorrow so I shall get marked A1 and I shall be leaving here a week next Friday with out something happens. I do not know where I shall land to and I am not troubling very much for it is as much about the same in the Army wherever you go. I am more fed up with the Army since I came from home as I ever was. It is one continual thing and here they muck us fellows about worse than recruits. We are never in one hut for 5 minutes together. We have been having very wet weather here lately but it is to be hoped we get a change before long as it will make harvesting bad.

I heard from West a few days ago he is keeping very well but from his letter he has been in the danger zone but is now back. He does not think the War is going to be over this winter but I think it will not last much longer as everybody seems fed up with the whole show and our heads seem to be making plenty of blunders and the Geries brass cannot agree with each other. I expect it will end in a draw but that would not bother me a deal and I don't expect it would you at Home and the Boys here are of the same opinion.

I hope Bill gets Home for a leave if possible but wherever he is he will be A1 and have very little to trouble and he will not have the pleasure of seeing France again. He seems to be getting on alright now and gets up of a afternoon so I expect he will start to get a little fatter.

I met Norman Gaskin Saturday and was out in camp with him Saturday and Sunday. He is only ten minutes walk from me but is at the recruits training camp. I was quite surprised to see him and you never mentioned anything in your letter. I was expecting him down tonight but the weather is bad so I shall see him tomorrow. Norman does not relish the Army very much and they keep all troops pretty well occupied in the Depot. This next week I have to do three fifteen miles march before I leave this Depot rather stiff for wounded troops. We had one Friday and about half of them fell out but they do not care how your wounds affect you. They think we are bits of machinery.

I must now be closing and I hope you are keeping well at Home and I hope you are going on alright with Holly's affair. I see the Burton papers with a small account in and about being put back for further trial at Derby. There is a fellow from Burton in my hut.

This leaves me A1

Love to all
x Walter x

LETTER DATED 22ND JUNE 1918 FROM WALTER POUNDS WHILE SERVING WITH THE BRITISH EXPEDITIONARY FORCE IN FRANCE

Dear Mother and Dad

Just a few lines to you hoping they find you in the best of health at Home. I was pleased to receive your letter today 22nd posted on the 12th it had been around France by the look of it. They had mistaken your K for T2 Group. So do not put K Group on just my numbers and Battery. It seems ages since I last heard from you but maybe others have gone astray it's the first I have received since writing and telling you of the medal. I was glad to hear Bill was at Home again and looking well, his stay at Duston was short so now he has to wait for further treatment but the stay at home should do him good. What Battery is Alf Boothway in? I just forget the Battery that took our Position over as we only stayed there four days before going out on rest. I would have liked to have seen him but may get a chance if I know his Battery on my return from here. I had forgotten he was in the RGA. I was surprised to hear of some of the older men leaving the Village. I should hardly think that Dad would have to go in any case he would not come out here. At present there seems no end to the War though the news this last few days are fairly bright. I am still having a decent time but this work of Learning is not in my line but I guess it will do me good after the course for there is a lot to learn in Artillery, so I am getting my mind on it while down here and learn what I can. I must ring off hoping the letter from here arrived safe this leaves me OK.

So with love to all, from Walter xxx PS just ask Bill to write

Army Records for Walter Pounds M.M.

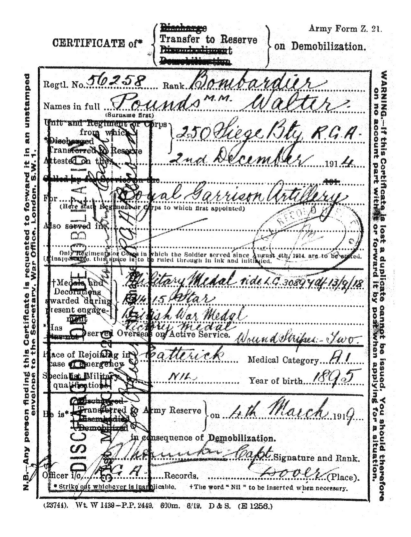

Mr. Derrick P.W. Pounds Eng

Serial No. RGA/151
Army Form B. 2067

NOTE.—The character given on this Certificate is based on holder's conduct throughout his military career.

Character Certificate of No. 56258 Rank Bombardier
Name Pounds M.M. Walter
  Surname.   Christian Names in full.
Unit and Regiment or Corps from which discharged } 25 Siege Battery R.G.A.

This is to certify that the ex-soldier named above has served with the Colours for Four years Three months, and his character during this period was very good; honest sober steady, intelligent and hardworking.

DeSausmarez Colonel Signature and Rank.

Transferred to Class "Z" Reserve Officer i/c R.G.A. Records. Dover Place.
Date of discharge 4-3-1919.

To safeguard the holder of this Certificate from impersonation it should be noted that, in the event of any doubt arising as to the bona fides of the bearer, reference should be made to the description, when he left the Colours, of the soldier to whom this Certificate was given, which is recorded on his Discharge Certificate (Army Form B. 2079, Serial No. ....), and should be in his possession.

Not Applicable

WARNING.—If this Certificate is lost a duplicate cannot be issued. You should therefore on no account part with it or forward it by post when applying for a situation, but should use a copy attested by a responsible person for the purpose.

NOTE.—This Certificate is to be issued without any alteration in the manuscript.

(A17624-P453) Wt. W3771/P4007 100,000 3/21 Sch. 41 D. D. & L. Forms/B2067/9

Awards Received by Walter Pounds M.M.

As noted earlier, during the First World War, Walter Pounds became a decorated soldier who was awarded the Military Medal (M.M.) for bravery, the British Army's second-highest commendation for valor, and three other medals with campaign ribbons, as shown on the following page.

Dad's Military Medal is shown top left (ref. ride. L.G.30897, 13/9/18); next is his 1914–1915 Star Medal, then his British War Medal, and then his Victory Medal. Walter Pounds's name tags are shown below his medals.

After discharge from army service on March 4, 1919, my father continued his gamekeeper and woodsman duties on the Ratcliff estate located around Newton Solney, Derbyshire, where he worked for almost fifty years.

While a resident in Newton Solney before, during, and after the Second World War, he was a special police constable and became a sergeant. For this volunteer service, my father received two police medals and three long service bars shown on the top right of the medals photo.

Mr. Derrick P.W. Pounds Eng

The Ratcliff Estate in Newton Solney

The Ratcliff estate included seven dairy farms, wooded areas, and large areas of cultivated land growing wheat, barley, root crops such as sugar beets, cow cabbage, turnips, mangles, and kale. In the 1920s to 1940s, Robert. F. Ratcliff, his brother, Percy W. Ratcliff, and Percy's spouse, Olive, occupied a majestic three-story mansion at Newton Park. Colonel R. F. Ratcliff CMG died in 1943, and upon the death of Percy W. Ratcliff in 1955, Newton Park was sold to pay death duties. In 1959 Percy's widow, Olive, moved nearby into "Cedars House" located opposite Church Lane, Newton Solney.

Newton Park became a hotel, and during Jarvis Hotels renovations in 1990, the game larder in the farm lane forecourt became guest room five. In 2013 Newton Park is a four-star hotel operated by Mercure and popular for wedding receptions.

In the years around 1950, the Ratcliffs had several house servants, including a cook, maids, a butler, a chauffeur, and as many as twelve gardeners who maintained the landscaped grounds. The Ratcliff families were leaders in the beer-brewing industry at Burton-on-Trent and were partners in the brewers Bass, Ratcliff, and Gretton Ltd., which became Bass Plc.

Walter Pounds's duties as gamekeeper for the Ratcliffs included rearing and preserving game, ornamental ducks, and fish stocks; organizing game shoots; training dogs; controlling vermin; and keeping poachers off the estate.

Work clothing was provided by the Ratcliffs, and new outfits were usually purchased every second year either from Cunningham's in Irongate, Derby; Ellis's, High Street; or Tarver's on Station Street, Burton. For daily estate duties year-round, my father generally wore a made-to-measure Harris tweed brown suit jacket with extra-large inside pockets, matching waistcoat, and plus-fours, along with shirt and tie, thick socks to the knee covered by gaiters, leather boots, and a Trilby hat. The tweed material was selected for camouflage so as to blend with light patterns formed in the woods. My father told of instances when owls and other birds quietly landed on his hat. This occurred while he was standing, like a post, in the woods during nightfall vigils, waiting and watching for poachers and vermin. There was a public footpath from Winshill through part of the Ratcliff estate, but no one was allowed on other parts of the estate except people who worked there or on the farms. Being the gamekeeper's son, I roamed freely on the estate, while anyone stepping off the public footpath or walking a dog without a lead attached could be charged and prosecuted for trespassing as indicated by the warning signs.

Walter Pounds provided the Ratcliff household with food supplies, including wild game and fresh hens' eggs. Our free-range chickens included Rhode Island reds, Holland blues, and bantam varieties. His woodsman's duties involved preparing new plantations and maintaining the woodlands' areas, including tree replanting where mature trees had been harvested. I enjoyed working in the woods helping my father. We would usually light a bonfire to burn the piles of rubbish produced in the clearing operations. He also maintained easy access along the rides through the woods by using a goshook and scythe. In order to mow effectively, it was necessary to sharpen the curved blade of the scythe with a foot-long grinding stone about every thirty minutes. We often used a two-man crosscut saw, which had an eight-inch-wide blade six feet long with a wooden handle at each end, to cut logs from fallen hardwood trees because chain saws and other power tools were not available. Brush and tree branches were tied into dozens of small bundles and sold, at one shilling each, for garden use to support peas and other climbing plants. Hand tools such as a goshook, slasher, machete, ax, and bow saw were used to clear alders and lay hawthorn hedges around the woods. A grafting spade, having a narrow long blade, was needed for planting spruce, fir, larch, oak, and other saplings. Many snowberry bushes, laurel, holly, juniper, boxwood, bayberry, and other broadleaf evergreen shrubs were planted to provide ground cover for game. The berries from these shrubs and bushes, as well as acorns, provided some winter feed for pheasants, which were also fed grain along the rides every morning.

Training Dogs

Vegetable and flower gardens surrounded the Walter Pounds family home at Bothy House located below Castle Hill about one-half mile southwest from Newton Solney. Behind a privet hedge starting forty yards from the house were free-range-chicken pens, ferret pens, and dog kennels. The three dog kennels had concrete floors that were swept with a stiff stable brush and washed daily as well as closed-in sleeping quarters filled with straw. The two dog kennels near our house were built side by side and each had a large window fitted with reinforced glass in the sleeping quarters.

There were two smaller doghouses, made of wood with solid floors and rounded roofs, located in the field just outside the perimeter of Bothy House's one-half-acre fenced property. These were enclosed inside a single barbed-wire fence to keep grazing animals away. The dogs occupying these houses had long, light chains attached to their collars and the doghouse. The dogs kept in circa 1940 to 1950 included Biddy, a black Labrador; two springer spaniels named Too and Fro; a Yorkshire terrier called Bess; and Flash, a curly coat black Labrador retriever. They were all purchased as puppies from trained pedigree parents.

Our dogs were fed on food scraps including bones and skim milk from the Newton Park kitchen and two types of dog biscuits that I also enjoyed. Fresh meat bones, bought from the butcher for one shilling a bag, were sometimes also fed to our dogs.

I do not remember any of our dogs ever being sick or having to be seen by a vet. Any tenderness around the ears was cured by an ear-drop solution dispensed from a glass medicine bottle.

Occasionally our dogs each ate a few mouthfuls of green grass that made them cough. The long grass, growing wild, was selected, picked, and eaten on their own initiative, and I never understood if this acted as a natural medicine.

The springer spaniels and Labradors were trained to keep at heel without a leash attached to their collars. When given the command, they would search, find, and carefully retrieve game that had been shot. They would retrieve game to an outstretched hand and would let go when you accepted it and rewarded the dog with a pat. It is vital that dogs used as retrievers develop a soft mouth so as not to damage the game. A rolled-up, dried rabbit skin was often used for training purposes. I was never allowed to throw wooden sticks for our dogs to retrieve.

To develop our dogs' retrieving skills, a pheasant's wing was tied to a long string and then dragged along the ground in a zigzag pattern up the field in front of Bothy House. At the end of the scent trail the wing would be hidden in a tussock, without our dogs seeing where. One dog would be released in the field and told to "go seek" with a direction command. The dog would search enthusiastically with nose to the ground, zigzagging along the scent trail, and usually found and retrieved the wing quickly. We would progressively increase the distance up the field where the wing was hidden and also change direction and crisscross the scent to try to fool our dogs. It was not always easy for the tracking dog to immediately find the wing, due to fresh scent from other animals being all over the field. Our dogs were trained to disregard the odors from the droppings of rabbits, cows, horses, and sheep in their focused search for the scent leading to the pheasant wing.

The dogs were broken of their normal tendency to run toward game the moment a shot had been fired, and when fully trained they only moved ahead when instructed. At first it was necessary to keep our dogs on leads, but once they remained steady when a gun was fired a lead was no longer used.

Pheasant and Partridge Shoots

Pheasants and partridges hatched in the shed incubators and reared in the pens around Bothy House were released on the estate in early summer, after attaching a tiny identification tag to one leg, when they could fly. There were also many nests of pheasants and partridges from wild stock that hatched broods of birds that grew up naturally on the estate. That's why game bird predators such as foxes, hawks and some owls were dealt with as vermin.

The pheasants were fed in the woods along the rides every day when the weather turned cold. On winter mornings a game bag would be filled with two large bowls of grain from our corn bins and taken out to each wood on the estate for scattering along the rides. A few days before pheasant shoots, sweet-smelling aniseed liquid was mixed with the pheasant feed grain. This was done in an effort to attract any pheasants that had strayed to return to the woods. Some roved outside the woods into root fields and hedgerows to feed. After spreading feed on the rides, I would whistle melodious notes that my father taught me. I then would hide to watch and count the number of birds coming to feed, reporting the totals seen in each wood to my father. Following a heavy snowfall, bundles of wheat and oat stalks in sheaves were split and spread along the rides. The pheasants were then able to search for grain above the snow.

The Ratcliff family, together with invited guests, usually started in September hunting game using double-barreled shotguns.

The regular guests at shoots on the estate during the mid-1940s included male and female members of the Thompson, Auden, and Forshall families plus Arthur Riley (the estate agent). The meadows, corn stubble, and root fields were driven first for partridges and hares. Sometimes the hunters with guns would walk with the beaters, but usually they would wait behind hedgerows. Some hawthorn hedgerows were cut to provide butts of person-sized higher sections every forty yards behind which a hunter hid, with shotgun at the ready, waiting for the game to pass. During such a drive in 1949, one of our springer spaniels was shot accidentally by an inexperienced hunter. My father cried.

During drives over solid ground, wild game including snipe and woodcock were also shot around the sewage farm at Etwall. Each wing of a woodcock has one tiny flight feather that is about one inch long and grows tucked close to each wing bone. Flight feathers from woodcock were in demand for use by artists.

Pheasant shoots usually involved about twelve invited hunters carrying twelve- or twenty-gauge shotguns. The hunters and their assistant observers stood at individual positions spread out in open fields around the wood in which the drives took place. Six-foot-long wooden sticks marked the place for each hunter to stand. The woods were driven by beaters during the pheasant shoots that peaked around Christmastime and continued into the new year. Beaters, usually young men from the village, would walk slowly through the wood in line and try to flush the pheasants toward the guns. The beaters were briefed before the pheasant shoots on the role they were expected to play and were sometimes given flags to wave. They were told to pause when pheasants started to fly so that the hunters had time to reload. Some pheasants usually took to the air when the beaters, armed with a wooden stick, started rattling the trees. Other game birds were disturbed when the dogs got close. The birds would try to fly high to other wooded areas over the heads of the hunters. The hunters were instructed to only shoot at birds passing overhead or behind their stand, never at the front or side since the pellets could carry to the beaters or other hunters. Some hunters completely missed their targets, and each hunter usually had two guns and an assistant to reload. Other game such as woodcock, hares, and rabbits would often be shot during the Christmas shoots.

A horse and cart were used to transport the shot game to the main entrance at Newton Park where it was sorted by Walter Pounds. A brace of pheasants was set aside on the stone steps near the front door for giving to each of the invited hunters. Remaining game was hung on meat hooks in the larder.

Hunting Rabbits Using Ferrets

Rabbits were classed as vermin because they could do so much damage to valuable fields of wheat, oats, barley, and sugar beets. Rabbits were therefore hunted using ferrets and purse nets, long nets, snares, leghold traps, .22-caliber rifles, and shotguns. Rabbits were a very important source of fresh meat, particularly during the war years. Rabbit meat was cooked in a variety of ways, but fried with onions was my favorite.

Walter Pounds bred and trained ferrets, as many as eight in a litter, both pure white with pink eyes and polecat gray and black varieties. Their home was in about twelve wooden pens raised off the ground chest high. The living areas of the pens were cleaned out using a shovel each morning after the ferrets had eaten and had returned to their sleeping quarters. The waste removed was often very smelly, and sawdust was used to dry up the wet areas of the pens and lime was spread on the waste.

The ferrets were well fed with kitchen scraps, skim milk, and other leftovers including fish heads from the Radcliffs' Newton Park. Handling was particularly important training for the young ferrets, and often they would squawk, scratch, and try to bite when handled. When the young ferrets had been trained and were grown up, many were sold each year to customers in Britain and Ireland. The gill (female) white ferrets, with or without some of their grownup young, were placed at the entrance to holes in rabbit warrens and would go down the holes to drive out any rabbits. Purse nets, each held with a wooden, six-inch peg pushed into the ground, were spread over all the rabbit holes in the warren to catch the rabbits when they tried to escape. On rare occasions there were not enough purse nets to cover all the hundred or so holes in a large warren. In such circumstances the rabbit escaping from one uncovered hole would dart back into a hole hopefully covered by a pegged purse net and was caught on entry into the hole. Father stopped breeding ferrets in the mid-1950s when many rabbits died after contacting a highly contagious viral disease called myxomatosis.

Hunting More Vermin

Hunting foxes using horses and hounds was not carried out on the Ratcliff estate. There was an influx of healthy foxes around Newton Solney every time there was an hunt meeting at nearby Bretby or Repton. These foxes were shot on sight as vermin since they caused damage that was not compensated by the hunt managers. Baited traps were set when necessary to catch foxes in each of the woods on the estate. The internal organs of rabbits were used as bait. These were poured into a shallow depression that was scraped out at the base of a tree and then covered with soil and leaves to deter flies. Evergreen branches were stuck in the ground, positioned close together in two rows extending out about four feet from the tree and bait to form a conical entrance about two feet wide. Two leghold traps were set and covered with fine soil inside the cone about one foot from the bait; each was secured using strong braided wire wrapped around the tree. The traps were checked every morning during the walk-around when the pheasants were fed along the rides cut through the woods. The alarm guns and barbed-wire trip wires, set taut about twelve inches above the ground, were checked at the same time for signs of poacher activities. If an alarm gun was heard to discharge, Dad always investigated, even in the middle of the night. He never took a firearm out at night, only carrying a walking stick or cudgel for protection.

Moles were also pests that Walter Pounds trapped. Their velvet skins were carefully removed, dried on a board and sold. The Reverend Jansen's booklet titled *A History of Newton Solney Church* refers to many payments in 1746 for catching and killing moles (page 11). Hundreds of moles were caught around Newton Solney most years in the late 1940s after causing havoc on farmland and in peoples' gardens and lawns. The steel spring trap, set for the mole on its run below ground level, killed the animal instantly. The spring trap was set after removing earth, by hand or using a small trowel, from a four-inch section of the run. The trap was positioned with the spring release plate in the center and its two curved arms straddling the mole tunnel. It was sometimes better to set the traps on a main run in a hedgerow as the tops of the trap were exposed if the tunnel was shallow and the cattle could knock it. The trap was then covered with grass and soil on top to keep light out of the tunnel. When the mole passed through the tunnel, the release plate would be contacted and the spring closed the arms, killing the mole. Dead moles were delicately skinned using a scalpel, and the pelts were stretched and pegged out to dry. Mrs. Olive Ratcliff had specialists in London tailor a fur coat using treated skins from several hundred moles Dad caught on the estate. Dad sold additional moleskins like other vermin pelts and game-bird feathers in bundles to furriers and other leather treatment specialists. In the late 1940s fox skins fetched one pound and badger skins thirty shillings. Tail feathers from cock pheasants sold for a penny.

Fishing on the River Dove

There were many grassland areas on the estate, including those facing Newton Park on both sides of the river and in front of the willow bush near where the river Dove meets the river Trent. Two punts, twelve feet long, four feet wide, were rowed across the rivers Trent and Dove on fishing trips and for hunting parties. Walter Pounds was responsible for the keys to the punts' chained locks, the long wooden oars, and the upkeep of the punts, which were painted battleship gray.

The clean water flowing in the river Dove made it a good river for fishing. On several occasions, while fishing with my father from the bank in the Willowed Osier bed, he caught large pike weighing between ten and twenty pounds. Eels up to three feet long were caught while fishing on the bottom just outside the Osier beds. We also caught other fish including perch, barbel, grayling, and (I think) bream in this stretch of the river Dove where the water was clear under normal river flows. My mother often prepared the pikes and eels for eating at our dinner table. The eels especially were delicious to eat. After skinning and chopping the flesh into one-inch sections, my mother cooked them in a milk and onion sauce.

Pikes were caught on triple hooks, strong line, and short heavy rods using live roach, up to six inches long, as bait. Roach were caught from the ponds below Bothy House for live bait during pike fishing on the river Dove. The two triple hooks were attached to the bait spaced three inches apart, using braided wire, with one hook only through the dorsal fin to give the bait mobility. The pike usually struck the bait broadside and then took it across the river before pausing to turn the bait to swallow it head first. The river Dove pike often fought like salmon, jumping out of the water after running and shaking on the line. When their energy had been sapped, they were taken out of the water using a gaff hook attached to a long wooden shaft that could reach into the water down the steep riverbank. Walter Pounds and his regular Saturday visitor Albert Hill were fishing for pike on either side of a large willow tree that was overhanging the River Dove in the Osier bed when two pikes struck each of their roach bait at almost the same time. I held the only gaff hook, and both pikes were landed successfully. On the way home across the meadow to the punt on the river Trent, I dragged the larger pike using the gaff hook. While dragging the big fish across the meadow, it had collected some grass and slime, so when I got the big fish in the punt my father told me to wash off the grass. During the washing operation I let the pike slip off the gaff hook into the Trent, and we never saw the big fish again.

Eels were caught fishing on the Dove River bottom with a lead weight as anchor and a single hook baited with large earthworms that were dug out of our garden. The migrating eels usually swallowed the whole thing with the hook caught deep in their inside, so the hook was also attached to braided wire to prevent the eel from biting off the hook. Eels bite aggressively so care is needed after landing to kill them quickly by cutting behind their gills using a sharp penknife. Eels can live for a long time out of water. Where the rivers Trent and Dove join there is a fine fishing spot at the tip of land we called the Point. We spent many enjoyable hours fishing successfully for red-finned roach close to the bank at the Point on the Dove side and in the strong currents as the waters from the two rivers mix.

Dad's stepbrother, Uncle Hardy, did not return home when expected one evening after using the Ratcliff punt to cross the river Trent to fish at the Point. Fearing the worst when Uncle Hardy had not returned in the punt at nightfall, the police were called. The police found my uncle at midnight still fishing at the

Point, his explanation being that he had caught ninety-nine fish and wanted to catch one more before returning home. My uncle was often slow at reacting to situations, particularly where self-discipline was required. Rumors indicate he received a dishonorable discharge from the army for, among other things, throwing a broom at his sergeant major.

    Close to the Point there is a concrete pillbox with slit-type openings built to protect up to about eight armed defenders of the river crossing below the Point during an enemy invasion. Numerous butterflies hibernated on the pillbox's inside walls and ceiling, and usually a few did not survive the hibernation period. Dead butterflies, collected from inside the pillbox, were used as bait or thrown into the river Dove. As they floated downstream, fish snapped them up on a day when our usual bait did not attract fish.

Ratcliffs' Other Hunting and Fishing Properties

The Ratcliffs also had hunting and salmon fishing rights on an estate near Andover, Hampshire, and trout fishing rights on the tiny river Blythe at Hamstall Ridware, Staffordshire. We often fished for pike and perch at Hamstall Ridware to protect the trout fishing. Large pike weighing over twelve pounds and perch weighing up to about three pounds were caught, using minnows as bait, in the deep pool below the Road Bridge.

The Ratcliffs also had hunting and fishing rights near Chittlehamholt, North Devon, where Mr. Scott was the ghillie, and on the 36,000-acre Dundonnell estate near Ullapool, Scotland. Walter Pounds visited both places for periods with the Ratcliff hunting and fishing parties, working several weeks each year before WWII with the resident staff. These persons included ghillie Hector Morrison and stalker Angus McDonald at Dundonnell Lodge during shooting and fishing expeditions for red deer, grouse, ptarmigan, capercaille, salmon, and sea trout.

Derrick Pounds met Angus McDonald and his spouse, both in their nineties but still active, on a visit to their cottage in 1959. Angus showed me where Walter Pounds shot a red deer stag, the antlers of which decorated our living room. Their cottage and gardens were located below a mountain near Dundonnell Lodge. My older sister, Winnie, remembers spending August and September at Dundonnell Lodge for ten consecutive years from

1922 to 1932, during which time my mother prepared the meals for the Ratcliff hunting parties. (In 1998 the Dundonnell estate, complete with Georgian manor, was purchased by lyrics writer Sir Tim Rice, famed for several musical hits including some with composer Lord Andrew Lloyd Webber.)

Special Constable Walter Pounds

Walter Pounds M.M. was a special police sergeant for over twenty-five years before, during, and for many years after the 1939–1945 war. For unpaid voluntary police duties he was provided with a complete police uniform with three white stripes on each sleeve to show his sergeant rank, a whistle, ebony truncheon, headgear, and cape rainwear. On hearing the air raid siren, he put on his uniform and cycled to the checkpoint at the Newton Solney village green. Other constables met there to receive instructions for a course of action to follow. My father had to put a bandage on his right leg when getting dressed. One night there were three separate air raid warnings, with all-clears in between, which required the fitment and removal of his police uniform and the long bandage while getting dressed and undressed three times.

Special police constables for South Derbyshire circa 1945. Walter Pounds is seated third from the right.

He regularly rode his 1930s three-speed police bicycle with lever brakes and twenty-eight-inch wheels from Newton Solney during nighttime excursions along the village lanes. These rides were to check that about twenty other constables living in nearby villages, who had volunteered for police duties, were at their assigned checkpoints at specific times.

The route my father cycled from Newton Solney to Repton, Milton, Ticknall, Hartshorne, Newhall, Bretby, Winshill, and Burton boundary by bicycle would have taken at least an hour under good conditions without any long stops on the way. One wet night, while following an alternative route, he lost control going down the steep hill into Repton from Bretby and crashed into a side of the wall by the waterfalls.

For his voluntary police service, Walter Pounds received two medals, and in 1945, 1953, and 1963 he received three long service bars to his police service medal while still working as head gamekeeper on the Ratcliff estate at Newton Solney.

In the 1940s the chief constable of Derbyshire, Colonel Horatio Rawlings, sometimes accompanied by Police Superintendent Hutchison, used to visit with my father and other police volunteer members of the local community around our home near Newton Solney. The police volunteers and Home Guard volunteer soldiers were trained in public security to provide resistance should the enemy invade. After the war, Colonel Rawlings and Superintendent Hutchison used to visit our home and go hunting with my father and other invited guests on the Ratcliff estate. The police chief's magnificent golden retriever hunting dog was boarded for several weeks' training by my father.

My mother sometimes prepared a meal for these guests before shoots on Saturday night for wood pigeons that roosted in the woods in the winter months and for young rooks at three rookeries around Newton Solney that were shot as they left their nests in early May.

The special police constables and Home Guard volunteer soldiers had a security checkpoint at the Newton Solney village green and for shelter used a large Spillers brand gamekeepers' hut parked on the grass verge opposite the Unicorn Inn. The hut was fitted with bunks, but it had no facilities and was not heated. The hut was substantially made with an "extra stout" wooden  floor, mounted on fourteen-inch-diameter cast iron wheels, fitted with "half-heck doors" on one end, and had a small window made to slide open. After the war, the hut, which had towing rings, was moved to our home at Bothy House and parked in the field under the ash tree just outside our boundary fence. We used it first to keep sports equipment, a soccer ball, cricket bat, and wickets, and also as a playroom for me and my friends on rainy days.

The hut was later converted into a chicken pen. Using chicken wire, a closed-in, eight-foot-long expansion was built with a wooden floor off the ground connected to the door. Fitted inside with a perch bar, the hut became a pen for turkeys that my father bred for sale at Christmastime. During a storm one night in December 1948, a broad branch from the ash tree fell down on the pen, leaving a hole in the chicken wire. This allowed a fox to enter during the early morning hours and kill three almost full-grown turkeys, each weighing about twenty pounds, by biting off their heads. The fox dragged one away from the pen and partially buried it under cow dung in the field about one hundred yards away toward Jubilee Wood. My father doctored this turkey, inserting a tiny amount of strychnine poison on the tip of a knife blade into a small incision made with his penknife into the breast of the turkey. Next morning the fox was found dead. It was skinned and the carcass and turkey remains buried.

Walter Pounds was very careful handling poison, always keeping the small bottle locked up when not being used. Whenever he took it out, it was wrapped in a long cotton cover, laced by string, and carried in the handkerchief pocket of his jacket. The cotton wrapping was added around the bottle after an incident when an unprotected glass bottle cracked, spilling poison and contaminating his smoking pipe that was inside the same jacket pocket. Preparing for a smoke, he put the pipe stem to his lips; detecting a bitter taste, he spat out the poison before suffering any lasting effects. When Walter Pounds moved from his Barrow-on-Trent bungalow retirement home to "The Limes" seniors' residence in Mickleover, he gave me strict instructions, which I followed, to return a small bottle of poison to the pest officer living near Findern.

Growing Vegetables

Walter Pounds grew enough potatoes and green vegetables to last his family all year, and I helped with the digging, planting, weeding, and harvesting from an early age. I helped in the garden until my father released me. He would say, "OK, you can now go and kick the bag of wind around," which is what he called a soccer ball. We had gardens all around the house with many flowering plants including chrysanthemums growing in borders. Flower cuttings and vegetable samples were submitted at the annual village flower and vegetable exhibition when prizes were awarded.

During the war, Dad also planted potatoes, onions, and green vegetables in the four pheasant aviaries located up the field from our house next to the Jubilee Wood. The potatoes for winter supply were stored in a wooden shed attached to our brick coalhouse. The dry potatoes were laid in a large pile on dry straw and covered with more straw. During cold nights, a paraffin-burning hurricane lamp was lit and hung inside the shed to take the chill out of the air to protect the potatoes from freezing. Green vegetables like brussels sprouts and cabbages were picked out of the garden in the winter months since snow and cold were never enough to damage the plants. In fact, some frost seemed to improve the flavor of brussels sprouts and winter cabbage. Wood pigeons would occasionally pay visits to our garden in winter and eat the brussels sprouts, sometimes whole, when they were unable to find acorns and other food due to snow cover.

Green beans, both dwarf and climbing varieties, were picked in large quantities during the short growing season. Those not needed immediately were trimmed, salted, and stored, sealed in large earthenware containers, to be eaten during the winter months. Large onions were stored on strings and hung to dry in one of the sheds, and the smaller shallots were pickled in vinegar and stored in large glass jars. I helped mother preserve in bottles other produce from our garden, including gooseberries, blackberries, raspberries, plums, and damsons. Fruit jams and jellies were prepared by my mother every year, and some table wine, for adults only, was made from wild elderberries and rowanberries on at least two occasions. Other produce such as tomatoes were canned at the end of the growing season using the kitchen facilities in the Village Recreation Club and special equipment shared with other members of the Women's Institute. Mrs. Olive Ratcliff was a patron of the Women's Institute, and my mother, Florence, was secretary of the village branch for a few years before her death at age fifty-eight from a cerebral stroke on July 30, 1952.

We picked wild mushrooms that grew in the fields around our home and ate them, after peeling them and frying them in bacon fat, either for breakfast or afternoon tea. The only mushrooms we ate grew quite quickly in grass land areas, often in the shade of trees, and were identified by their white caps, pinkish ribbed underside, and particular odor. They were easy to peel. To keep out the light and hence make mushrooms grow faster, tufts of grass were usually plucked and spread over small mushrooms that we found. The fresh grass soon changed color so there was no problem finding the covered mushrooms a day later after they had grown.

There were three large walnut trees near our home that produced edible nuts in the autumn. Edible nuts were also harvested from a sweet chestnut tree growing in the park field close to home. Before chestnuts were eaten they sometimes were roasted on a fork, but usually in a pan held over the fireplace. Beech and hazelnuts were also collected from trees growing in the woods on the estate. As part of the war effort, rose hips were picked from wild roses growing in hedgerows to produce special medicines.

Food rationing did not end until several years after World War II, but we were able to get around shortages with substitutes. Bananas were not available in Britain during the war.

Planting Trees and Evergreen Shrubs

In the mid-1940s, my father planted many evergreen shrubs, including junipers, boxwood, and bayberry below the larch plantation in the Home Wood. The bushes grew well in the richly composted soil. Permission was given to a wreath-making person from Burton and a foliage merchant from Nottingham to prune away uneven growth from evergreens growing in the woods on the estate. A fee of five shillings was charged for every sheet, bundle, or bag of evergreen clippings removed. This permission was canceled when they were caught leaving with a lorry load without paying the required fee at the estate office. My father planted many fir trees at the top of the Home Wood, but there was a problem with people stealing them at Christmastime. The thieves usually took only the top few feet of the trees. It took many years of new growth for the trees to recover their shape. He caught people with the tops of fir trees in their possession, and their names and addresses were recorded. However, Percy Ratcliff was reluctant to prosecute the offenders, who were usually the heads of large Winshill families.

Rhododendrons, planted by my father, grew profusely underneath the large oak, beech, and ash trees in the Home, Jubilee, Back Longford, and Ranglings Woods. These evergreens produced magnificent flowers that released an intoxicating fragrance during spring and summer. Some rhododendron flowers were almost as big as footballs, and the bushes were over six feet tall. Planted about ten feet apart, they were close enough to provide a good canopy cover for both animals and birds. Underneath this canopy at ground level there were thick layers of leaf mold without any vegetation growing. One could see clearly underneath the rhododendrons during daylight hours when crouched or laying flat to the ground. Many types of songbirds built their nests in these shrubs, including thrush, blackbird, finches, warblers, wrens, and chiffchaffs. Mistle thrush, woodpecker, and jay nests were common in the taller trees, the jay being considered a pest because they were known to steal eggs from other birds' nests. The chorus of wonderful sounds produced by different bird species reached its peak during early summer when cuckoos also visited.

Walter Pounds's records show that in 1935 he planted 900 larch and 450 Scotch and Austrian pine trees at the Castle end of the Jubilee Wood, and 250 rhododendron and 100 box bushes at the lower end.

In March 1949, I helped Dad with the planting of many small oak trees in the Castle Wood and thirty-five rhododendron bushes near the road. The oaks grew, protected with wire netting, as replacements for the large beech and other hardwood trees that were harvested and carted away by timber merchants during the early 1940s. Daffodils and bluebells grew in abundance among the bracken on the north slope of this wood. The bulbs from these springtime flowers multiplied profusely, and pheasants and squirrels ate any bulbs developing near the surface. Gray squirrels were shot on sight while red squirrels, rarely seen, were never harmed.

Father's Other Notes

Walter Pounds M.M. recorded, throughout his life, the highlights of daily events by writing in large ledgers and small diaries. He was always focused on his responsibilities and estate work. His entry in one tiny diary on March 28, 1935, reads, "son born at 4:30." He also recorded my birth on the same date in another diary as "baby born" followed by "115 rats killed at Bladon farm." Bess, our Yorkshire terrier, was very quick at catching and killing rats.

Another example is an entry, copied on the next page, that he made on Saturday, May 21, 1927, in a "Boots"-type legal-size ledger that noted Lindbergh's feat, without writing the pilot's name. He wrote, "an American flew from New York to Paris in 36½ hours, landed in Paris Saturday night 9:20 p.m."

My father's notes taken from his police diary give details of an encounter that took place on November 5, 1961, when he was sixty-six years old:

"Hearing shots in Castle Wood between 10:30 am and 11:00 am I was in the bottom end of the Park there were two more shots at the top end of the Jubilee Wood. I went half way out in the Park where I could look through a ride cutting the wood in half. I saw two men on the far side. I went to the top of the wood and again saw two men on the far side of the wood. Cutting through the top of the wood I heard voices say 'what have we got.' On coming to the rail fence I saw four men, a bunch of pheasants and two guns lying on the grass. The men were bending down looking at the kill. I said what are you lot up to, you know you have no rights here. I got over the rail fence and while I was getting over the men made a grab for the guns and pheasants and rabbit. The man with the 12 bore said stand back or he would blow my bloody head off and I would not be the first. I advanced towards him showing my Police Badge and told him (since) I was a Police Officer; he would get into trouble if he shot me. One of the men on his left said, "He means it" and they all started backing away. As I advanced towards them the man with the 12 bore bent down and said if you come any further he would blow off both my 'B' legs. He was swinging the gun from left to right as I walked towards him. At that moment they all turned about and ran off towards Bladon Top Wood. I gave chase blowing my Police whistle when on the top of the hill they came to a stop. After going a few more yards I saw the top of a Police helmet and was pleased. When I saw the Police I told them that they had threatened to shoot me. I pointed to the fair haired man and he said it was only in fun, as the gun was not loaded." I found other notes that indicate that the four men were summoned to Repton Police court where on 7th March 1962 they were fined.

I witnessed many other instances of my father's bravery and courage under difficult circumstances as he challenged poachers and unauthorized intruders on the Ratcliff estate. Some of these encounters progressed from scuffles to assault with real violence.

My father and I were ferreting for rabbits at the top of the Ranglings Wood when we saw about ten persons walking across nearby grassland. We knew they were not supposed to be there so my father decided to investigate. My father went out of the wood unarmed. While challenging these men he was surrounded and then knocked to the ground, falling flat on his back. I shouted out loud and fired a warning shot with my father's .22-caliber rifle high over their heads from a distance of about fifty yards. They turned and saw me behind the hawthorn hedge before taking off over the hill to return to the public footpath. My father did not indicate that he was badly hurt. The group of intruders that knocked my father to the ground apparently included a local boxer, who later became the British champion.

Walter Pounds was a keen sportsman who played cricket for Newton Solney for many years. In 1922 he got a hat trick, three wickets with consecutive balls, against Stapenhill while playing on the Trent grounds. In 1923 Newton Solney won the Burton Brewery Cup. During the final game, Dad hit three sixes, scoring eighteen runs from consecutive balls while playing against the Bass Brewery team. He hit the next ball hard straight up and was caught out by the wicket keeper.

Dad batted right-handed but held the bat contraire to the norm with his left hand below and the right hand at the top of the handle. After the war I helped my father and others rebuild the two small cricket pavilions in the Newton Solney cricket field where homes were built in the 1960s.

MOON RISES 10.51 p.m.
MOON SETS 5.46 a.m.

MAY, 1927.

SUN RISES 4.4
SUN SETS 7.50

20 FRIDAY (140-225)

Turned Pheasants out of Pens
6 Hens 1 Cock Spent
14 " 2 Soft Wood.
12 " 2 Park Spinney
6 " 1 Soft Wood,
last lot of Pheasants Sat.
Total number Sat 1,025
Partridges down to date 52

Bought 3.00.
Wild 1.9.
Pheasant 60
Pens 1.66

21 SATURDAY (141-224)

American flew from New York
to Paris in 33⅓ Hours
landed in Paris Saturday night 9.20 p.m.

5ᵗʰ April 1977.
Shooting
Is a dangerous game for the untrained, before you learn to shoot Try and learn distance for it plays a big part when to fire, so much is lost and wooded if the shooter has not learned distance and always respect a Gun or Rifle, they are not playthings, when Guns are in line you must not fire left or right, you must fire forward, over head, or behind, then you will inflict no damage to other Guns In walking up game you must keep a straight line and it is better to mark your kill and keep on walking and go back with dogs for the pick up, always clean your Guns after using, even though you have not shot, sweat from your hands if left will rust, if putting Gun pegs in allow 30 yds between pegs if your stand is on open ground place plaited Hurdles In line with your other Guns, Duck shooting and Teal are inclined to go upward so if you aim for the head you will always get a kill, but all shooting depends on your own skill.

The Hedgehog
Is nearly the worst enemy of any gamekeeper for he will take the eggs while the birds are laying also when they are sitting he is capable of climbing trees and a first class Swimmer he will attack the hens in coops also when game is hatching Just before I retired The gardener told me of Pheasant eggshells on the path he said it was Jackdaws I went to inspect and

63

Mr. Derrick P. W. Pounds Eng

Walter Pounds kept records of his working expenses in account books, which Percy William Ratcliff reviewed and signed off on every month. These also make for interesting reading.

For example, as the following shows, my Dad's wages in 1935 were two pounds fifteen shillings each week, and five gallons of beer cost one pound, six shillings, and eight pence.

The last item on the bottom right states, "Paid W. Pounds Snr [Dad's father] 17 shillings for painting punt 2 coats."

On "Shoot day," September 7, ten beaters were paid three shillings each and five beaters were paid six shillings each for disturbing game birds for hunters to shoot at. It was usual to give adult beaters double the reward that teenage beaters received.

Walter Pounds circa 1912.

Barbara, Florence, Winnie and Derrick Pounds (in pram) circa 1937.

Father's Other Notes

Walter and Florence Pounds circa 1950.

Walter Pounds M.M. was an expert outdoorsman, marksman, trapper, woodsman, fisherman, and gardener. His father at Newton Solney and grandfather who lived at Milton and Repton had coached him well.

Walter Pounds won the first-prize bottle of whiskey several times during the annual Christmas shoot after hitting the bull's-eye at twenty-five yards on the Newton Solney village indoor rifle range. His only rifle was a .22-caliber, single-shot, lever-operated BSA (Birmingham Small Arms) serial 14185 that he carried every day during patrols on the Newton Park estate.

In 1977 my father wrote the following notes. The titles are "Shooting," "Purse netting for rabbits," "Long netting," "Hedgehog," "Hunting Red Deer," "Snaring Rabbits," and "Sparrow Hawk—deadly hunter."

"Shooting": It is a dangerous game for the untrained, before you learn to shoot try and learn distance for it plays a big part when to fire. So much is lost and wounded if the shooter has not learned distance and always respect a gun or rifle, they are not playthings. When guns are in line you must not fire left or right, you must fire forward, overhead or behind, then you will inflict no damage to other guns. In walking up game you must keep in a straight line and it is better to mark your kill and keep on walking and go back with dogs for the pickup. Always clean your guns after using even though you have not shot, sweat from your hands if left will rust. If putting gun pegs in allow 30 yards between pegs. If your stand is on open ground place plaited hurdles in line with your other guns. Duck shooting and teal are inclined to go upwards so if you aim for the head you will always get a kill, but (success in) all shooting depends on your own skills.

"Purse netting for Rabbits": "This is quite a skillful operation and most of the time you are on your knees. You require a good trained dog also ferrets. The dog will tell you if the warren contains rabbits. No talking is important. The nets must be pegged from the back, with the mesh covering the hole. Any holes you cannot net should cover up with soil. Once caught, it is best to take the rabbit out (before breaking its neck), as you are liable to break the mesh. If the ferrets get laid and the rabbits will not bolt you use the line ferret, which should be a hob (male). The line should have a yard knot so as to let you know how near you are to the ferrets. A trained dog will go around the warren and start scratching (the ground) over the location of the rabbit and ferret confrontation. When digging (at these locations) you should be on top of the kill so be careful where you put the grafting tool (spade). You should collect and count your nets before going out and finishing (before you return).

The vicar went (rabbiting) one day with the keeper. They had caught two; the third got through the net. The keeper shouted, damn and blast. The vicar said John, get down on your knees and pray and thank the Lord, for we have two out of three."

"Long Netting": "It is a serious and time study and no good that amateurs trying it since you have so many components to understand. The weather is the most important problem (since) you must have the wind blowing towards the net; the night must be dry and no moon. You must inspect the fields (beforehand) and no cattle or horses should be present.

The man who runs the net must know his job, as you can, if not careful, drop too much (net) at a time. The pegger will give

2 sharp pulls if this happens on the top cord, which the pegger holds at all times holding close to the body. After the first peg he will measure 7 yards, the bottom line (cord) is held with a half twist the same as the top, if too much slack you can on the top line give an extra twist. When the man who runs (the net) out sees the pegger getting close he will leave to drive in, taking a wide swing. When he is at the back of the field he will throw a lighted match into the air as a signal he is going to start driving in. The pegger kneels low at the (last) point of pegging with his hand on the top line so he can tell when the first rabbit is in the net where (at which point) he will run down, break (the rabbits) the neck and throw at the back (behind the net) after putting the mesh straight. This amounts to 10 pegs for 75 yards of netting. After the kill taking the net down (involves removing the end steel peg) and undoing the first (wooden) peg pulling the top line towards the body to make the mesh fall inside between top and bottom (cords). Pick (collect) up (the netting with the cords threaded) on the finger and then transfer to the (steel) peg (so) then you are ready for the next set. You need to have (require) a (large) inside pocket (in your jacket) to hold the (wooden) pegs which must be held tight to (the) body and they must be strong."

"<u>Hedgehog</u>": The hedgehog is nearly the worst enemy of any gamekeeper for he will take the eggs while the birds are laying also when they are sitting. The hedgehog is capable of climbing trees and also a first class swimmer. He will attack the hens in coops also when game is jugging. (resting close together on the ground). Just before I retired the gardener told me of pheasant (egg) shells on the path he said it was jackdaws. I went to inspect and I could tell it was the prickly lad (hedgehog). Looked around and found the pheasants nest with 10 eggs all covered in yoke which I replaced with dummies (pot eggs). I knew prickly lad would be back at night, so I set 100 yards of rabbit netting away from the holly bushes where I thought they were resting, and got the gardener to look the first thing in the morning. He came back to breakfast and reported he had cut two hedgehog throats and left them (in the net). So I did get 10 pheasant eggs (for rearing purposes).

<u>Hunting Red Deer</u>" at Moy Lodge, Scotland: " 8 o'clock in the morning, a wet morning, after climbing the first guernie, which is a piece of land between two mountains, after one hour stalk we located 2 Stags with about 20 hinds. The Rifleman, after a bit of luck, shot both Stags, I used to go (went) and put a shot in the neck to stop any suffering. Both beasts were 9 pointers weighing 15½ stone each. The first thing you do is pierce the neck to get rid of hot blood, then you garllok taking all the inside out pulling any fat from the intestines, generally. The Stalker keeps a red hosiery and all fat is put in, and the body is stuck with a wooden pin. One takes the horns; the other places rope around the hind legs for holding on steep ground so the beast cannot knock you off your legs. We get the first beast down to the Pony Man, and climbed back for the second, which we got to the pony track. At that point the stalker said, 'Sir, this beast must stay on the moor until daybreak.' The reply (from Percy Ratcliff) was 'I want both Stags to be in the larder tonight' and (Percy Ratcliff) then walked back to Moy Lodge. The Stalker said, 'Pounds what shall we do'? I said 'we will drag the bugger', so we set off across the open moor and after 3 hours dragging we arrived back (at Moy Lodge). If ever you felt sick at looking at a deer now was the time. After landing (arriving) at the lodge we had them both to skin, as the skins come off better than when cold, they are then slung on beams, ready for sawing down the middle. If the Rifleman wants the horns I make a fire outside and take all the meat from the head leaving the face of the skull attached to the horns."

On the following page are Dad's original handwritten notes that are transcribed above.

Father's Other Notes

MOY LODGE   4th April 1977
1922   RED DEER 2, 9 Pounds WHEIT 15½ Stone

8 o'clock in the morning a wet morning after climbing the first Gurrie which is a piece of land between 2 mountings, after 1 Houre Stalk we located 2 Stags with about 20 Hinds. The rifle man after a bit of luck shot both Beasts, I used to go and put a stob in the neck to stop any suffering. The first thing you do is piece the neck to get rid of hot blood Then you gillet, taking all the inside out, pulling any fat from the intestines, generally. The Stalking keeps a Red humming, all fat is put in, and the body is stitch with a wooden pin. one takes the Horns, the other man places rope round hand leg for holding, on steep ground so as the beast cannot knock you off your legs We get the ferst beast down to the pony turn, and climbed back for the second which we got to the pony track, at that point the Stalker said, Sir this beast must stay on the moore until daybreak the reply was I want both Stags to be in the larder to night, and walked back to the Moy lodge The Stalker said Pounds what shall we do I said we will have to drag the bugger, so we set off across the open moor and after 3 hours dragging we arrived back. If ever you felt sick at looking at a Deer now was the time, after landing at the Lodge we had them both to skin, as the Skins comes of better than when cold, they are then slung on beams, Ready for Sawing down the middle. If the Rifle man wants the Horns I make a fire outside and take all the meat from the head leaving the face of the Skull attached to Horns   W. Reinolds M.M.

(a Scotsh while skinning)

"**Snaring Rabbits**": Snaring is a good method of educating rabbits from poachers. It makes them not so bold. Home made snares are the best, you require two pegs, four strands (of bronze wire about two feet long), one peg is (held) firm the other you place between the thumb and finger then stretch and twist (the wire). You will find the snare reduced (in length) from when you started. When a rabbit is caught he will pull the snare to its original length. (so it is necessary to retwist the wire before reusing). Do not set snares where there are livestock and get well away from Woods and never when there is a moon. If you are setting 100 snares every 10 you should reverse, so when you pick up it will save your legs. Elder is a good wood to use, as it is light and when picking up it will stand a tap with the foot. The snare should be set on the jump. The width (height) should be four fingers from the ground. One half hitch around the peg, easy for taking off."

On most days, Walter Pounds carried only his single-shot, .22-caliber, lever-action BSA rifle during patrols while walking every day in the woods and along hedgerows around the estate. Poachers often set snares for rabbit and hares, usually on tracks passing through hedgerows, and he searched for and removed any found on the estate. My father also hand searched poachers apprehended trespassing on the estate and confiscated any items that were potential threats to game. He used to patrol the Ratcliff estate on foot seven days a week looking and listening for signs of poachers, and he fearlessly challenged any unauthorized intruders. There were footpaths crossing the estate between Winshill, Newton Solney, and Repton for walkers to use, but these provided only a narrow corridor that my father enforced. Persons trespassing on the estate were often searched, and items such as traps, snares, catapults, guns, or other weapons were confiscated. Dogs for running down game were also taken away. This was done despite expressions of great distress from the owners.

Walter Pounds also had four shotguns: a double-barreled ten-gauge hammer "duck" gun, a double-barreled twelve-gauge, a double-barreled .410-bore, and a single-barreled folding .410-bore. These were kept either in our sitting room gun case that had a lockable glass door or on overhead racks and in a gun case at one end of our large brick-based wooden shed. The shed had two large metal and wooden bins, each fitted with heavy sloping covers that were hinged at the back, for storing grains for feeding pheasants and poultry and two varieties of dog biscuits. The shed had a fireplace and was used for tool and equipment storage, including incubators for egg hatching, traps, snares, and purse and long nets. Dad also kept powder, shot, and equipment for recharging shotgun shells. The shed was locked every night and the large key hidden in a horseshoe over the door.

My father told me, to emphasize the danger of improper use of a firearm, how he accidentally shot a deer while working at Windsor Great Park on the estate of King George V. He had been assigned by the head gamekeeper to stop the deer grazing on young wheat growing in fields next to a wooded area. All the deer but one stag were easily kept away from the wheat field and would stay away when driven back into the woods. However, one adult stag kept returning to graze on the young wheat so Dad thought that more drastic scare tactics were necessary. He fired a shot over the deer's head. Unfortunately, the big deer raised its head as my father fired and the bullet killed the deer instantly.

Dad instructed me how to safely use a firearm, and from an early age I used a single-shot, bolt-action, Belgian-made, .22-caliber rifle almost every day. I would rarely go out in the woods on the estate without carrying it under my arm, ready for immediate use on vermin or food for the family. The packets of .22 rifle bullets said "dangerous within one mile," and from an early age I was taught to respect the dangers of firearms and the safety procedures to follow. These included how to carry a gun properly and the importance of keeping the barrel free of obstructions. You only fire when you know the area behind the target is clear, and you never leave a live bullet or empty case in a gun when you have finished using it. The types of .22 bullet used included "silent" shorts, long solid rimfire, long dum-dum hollow nose, and birdshot that was practically useless for other than scaring birds away. I was taught never to point a firearm at a person even if you know the gun is not loaded. I was also taught to never pull the trigger of a firearm when indoors even though you believe no bullet is in the breach, unless of course you are target shooting on a firing range. We kept no loaded firearms in our house even during the war years, and never had a revolver-type firearm. Dad advised that it is necessary to always clean inside the barrel after firing .22 birdshot since the charge contaminates the spiral grooves in the bore of the rifle. He preferred to use the short bullets for rabbits and the longs for larger vermin. Dad rarely used dum-dums since the flattened bullet produced a large exit hole, damaging the pelts on fur-bearing animals. Headshots were always targeted to obtain the maximum effect with the minimum of suffering, and in the case of rabbits, headshots were necessary, especially over rabbit warrens. I have witnessed numerous, probably hundreds, of experiences where a rabbit shot in the head with a .22, instantly falls over dead on its back. It raises a twitching hind leg in the air without any more movement after about two seconds.

"**<u>Sparrow Hawk—deadly hunter</u>**": "I was rearing pheasants on the wood side and had seen the hen sparrow hawk flying over I had looked for the nest previous that morning looking over a tall scotch fir I noticed a stick protruding. Not being a good tree climber, I waited for the under-keeper to come to breakfast and asked him to climb the tree. As he was half way up the hen bird flew off and through an opening I fired and killed her. I said (to the under-keeper) you wait and try and get the cock bird while I go to breakfast. I came back after 20 minutes and he (the under keeper) told me that the cock bird had been to the nest three times but could not get a shot being too quick. So I sat (and waited) the cock bird came again but was in like a flash and came over my head.

Glancing back I thought I saw a movement in an elder bush (and took) a chance shot that killed the cock bird. My under-keeper climbed (the tree) again and shouted down there were four dead small birds on the edge of the nest, (but) you could not name (identify) them as they were plucked with heads off. That was in twenty five minutes, so how many birds would he killed during the day is anyone's guess to feed four young sparrow hawks. The male (cock) bird strikes like lightning, the hen not so quick."

Father's Other Notes

The Sparrow Hawk   April 3 1977
Deadly hunter

I was rearing pheasants on the wood side. And had seen the hen Sparrow hawk flying over I had look for the nest previous that morning looking over a tall scotch furr. I noticed a stick protruding not being a good tree climer. I waited for the under Keeper to come to breakfast and asked him to climb the tree as he was half way up the hen bird flew off and through an opening I fired and killed her I said you wait and try and get the cock bird while I go to breakfast. I came back after 20 minuets and told me the cock bird had been to the nest 3 times but could not get a shot being too quick, so I sat the cock bird came again but was in like a flash and came over my head, glansing back I thought I saw a movement in a elder bush a chance shot I killed the cock bird My under keeper climed again and sholid down that there were 4 dead small birds on the edge of the nest you could not name them as they were plucked with heads off That was in 25 minuets so how many birds would be killed during the day is any ones guess to feed 4 young sparrow Hawks The male bird strikes like lighting, the hen not so quick

            W Pounds. MM.

Percy W. Ratcliff died on February 21, 1955, at age seventy-seven. His will instructed that all members of the estate staff receive one year's wages on his death, irrespective of the number of years worked. My father's wage when Mr. Ratcliff died was 390 pounds per year before taxes. There was no overtime pay, although he worked hard and was on call every day of the week. My Dad did not receive any estate pension after working fifty years for the Ratcliff family; however, lived a happy, healthy life into his mid-nineties during retirement years.

Walter Pounds M.M. and His Pound_ Ancestors

Walter Pounds's great grandfather Thomas Pound_ was also gamekeeper and woodsman serving from circa 1840 to 1885 on the estates of Sir Francis Burdett at Ramsbury, Wiltshire, and Foremarke, Derbyshire. Thomas Pound_ died age seventy-two and was buried at St. Saviour's Church, Foremarke, on August 10, 1885. His Pound_ family grave with inscribed headstone is at the right rear of the tiny churchyard under a yew tree, in which pheasants go to roost.

Thomas Pound (on pony), who was born in 1813, and sons John, James, Arthur, and my great-grandfather William Pound outside Foremarke Hall circa 1870. All five men worked on the Foremarke estate.

"Abide ye there while I come round unto thee" was a commonly spoken command delivered by Thomas Pound (died 1885) to trespassers apprehended on the other side of hedgerows during patrols on horseback around the Foremarke estate.

The Foremarke Hall—four stories high—was a stately home built in 1760 by Francis Burdett's (1770–1844) father, Robert. In the 1990s it became a boarding and day school for 450 boys and girls ages three to thirteen. Francis's son Baronet Robert Burdett (1835–1895) inherited the estate in 1844, which had been owned by the family for centuries, since 1327 listed as the Burdett game park. St. Saviour's Church, built by the Burdett family on the Foremarke estate in 1662, has a large dilapidated Burdett burial site on the right-hand side about the middle of the small church graveyard a few feet forward from the gravestone of my Pound ancestors, which on my last visit in 2001 was in pristine condition. The nicely engraved Pound headstone is full with names; however, Thomas is not listed because, I suspect, when he died in 1885 there was no more room for my great-great-grandfather's name to be engraved.

During a visit to Foremarke with my father around 1980, the gamekeeper walked with us around the estate and among other things showed us about eight Viking graves associated with the arrival of four Viking armies in Repton in AD 873, which brought the Anglo-Saxon kingdom of Mercia to an end. The unmarked graves were just mounds of soil a few inches high about six feet long with out-of-line random spacing of graves pointing in several directions. According to the gamekeeper, the soldiers had been buried where they had fallen in full battle gear, and it was forbidden to touch the grave sites, which were in an area of a wood among young trees. In 1982 a major archaeological dig around Repton's St. Wystan's Parish Church unearthed a Viking burial mound in the present Vicarage garden. Two hundred Viking warriors were found buried there, together with forty-nine women of Anglo-Saxon build. It is rather extraordinary that the only known Viking burials in the country should be within a few miles of each other.

In January 1989 Dad wrote me a note saying that *"my mother died when I was 6 years old and is buried close to the entrance (of St. Mary's Parish Church) after which dad had an housekeeper. I worked at the Castle for two years as Butler's Help where I had breakfast and tea. The butler used to allow me 5 minutes to run to school (in Newton Solney) for that I got 5 shillings a week and a golden half sovereign at Christmas. Saturdays I used to have my lunch at Garets(?) and help in the joinery shop & clean boots, weeded the garden paths. When I left school (Newton primary) Dad put me to Game Keepering at 5 bob a week. I should have been a shefe(chef)".*

I have very happy memories of my father Walter Pounds M.M. while growing up in Newton Solney, and he taught me a lot. Fried egg, with bacon, mushrooms, and bread, fried to a crisp in bacon fat, was my normal breakfast for many years. Occasionally Dad used to give me delicious-tasting small portions of his fried egg after I had eaten my share.

I used to enjoy riding on the crossbar of Dad's 1930s policeman's bicycle (that in 2013 I still have), with him peddling, on daily visits to Newton Park house to collect, in two big metal buckets hanging from the handlebars, skimmed milk and kitchen scraps to feed our dogs and ferrets. Dad taught me how to handle, without getting bitten too often, polecat and white ferrets that he bred. He also taught me to train dogs and set alarm guns to detect intruders in the estate woods. Among several other things Walter Pounds taught me so I could provide food for the table were the safe use of rifles and other firearms to hunt wild game and how to set nets, traps, and snares for vermin and wild animals. Dad was very clever using hand tools for repairing things including my shoes, which he taught me how to polish based on his army and earlier training. While in the army, he used to run in competitions in his bare feet until his sergeant arranged to get Dad proper running shoes.

Dad remained physically active into his early nineties, maintaining a large flower and very productive vegetable garden around his bungalow in Barrow-on-Trent before selling in 1988 after moving to "The Limes" retirement home in Mickleover.

The Passing of Walter Pounds M.M. at Age Ninety-Six

In January 1991, my ninety-six-year-old father, Walter Pounds M.M., suffered a stroke after being driven all around Derby for hours in a hospital minivan during a traffic-blocking major snowstorm. He had been examined at the Pastures Hospital that morning for blackness in a little toe on one foot, was released, and was put aboard the hospital minivan along with other patients for the ride home. Dad's residence at Mickleover was a short distance away, but for some unknown reason the driver dropped my father off last. My sister, Winnie, and brother-in-law, Harry, found Dad slumped in his chair and rushed him back to Pastures Hospital. On February 13, 1991, son Mark and I flew on British Airways BA 214 to visit with him. Although Dad was still alert, could talk, and able to grip my hands firmly, he was confined to bed, and he was not fully responding to treatments. The young lady doctor told me privately that it was unlikely my dad would fully recover and sadly that his earlier quality of life would not return. Mark and I returned to Canada on March 1, with both flights involving landings in Boston since few people were traveling due threats associated with the first Gulf war.

My father died peacefully. While in a coma he just slowly stopped breathing in his ninety-seventh year on March 15, 1991. Two uniformed policemen stood at attention at St. Mary's, Newton Solney, church door and thirty-one attended his funeral service on Thursday, March 21, conducted by Rev. G. Goodall. The service included Psalm 23, "The Lord's my shepherd, I'll not want…"; the lesson and the address; the hymn "Onward Christian Soldiers…"; more prayers; and a final hymn, "The day thou gavest, Lord, is ended…"

Walter Pounds M.M. was buried in a solid ash coffin with brass handles on Thursday, March 21, 1991, in the family grave located near the gate at the Trent Lane end of the footpath through St. Mary's, Newton Solney, graveyard.

Made in the USA
Charleston, SC
06 September 2013